TABLE OF CONTENTS

Top 20 Test Taking Tips

1. Carefully follow all the test registration procedures

2. Know the test directions, duration, topics, question types, how many questions

3. Setup a flexible study schedule at least 3-4 weeks before test day

4. Study during the time of day you are most alert, relaxed, and stress free

5. Maximize your learning style; visual learner use visual study aids, auditory learner use auditory study aids

6. Focus on your weakest knowledge base

7. Find a study partner to review with and help clarify questions

8. Practice, practice, practice

9. Get a good night's sleep; don't try to cram the night before the test

10. Eat a well balanced meal

11. Bring a set of ear plugs; the testing center could be noisy

12. Wear comfortable, loose fitting, layered clothing to the testing center; prepare for it to be either cold or hot during the test

13. Arrive to the test early; be prepared to wait and be patient

14. Eliminate the obviously wrong answer choices, then guess the first remaining choice

15. Pace yourself; don't rush, but keep working and move on if you get stuck

16. Maintain a positive attitude even if the test is going poorly

17. Keep your first answer unless you are positive it is wrong

18. Check your work, don't make a careless mistake

The English Test

The English portion of the EXPLORE will have questions about underlined portions of text, with possible replacements as answer choices. Read the text four times, each time replacing the underlined portion with one of the choices. While reading the choices, read the sentence before, the sentence containing, and the sentence after the underlined portion. Sometimes an answer may not make sense until you read the following sentence and see how the two sentences flow together. While reading the text, be sure to pause at each comma. If the comma is necessary the pause will be logical. If the comma is not needed, then the sentence will feel awkward. Transitional words should create smooth, logical transitions and maintain a constant flow of text.

Some questions will be concerning sentence insertions. In those cases, do not look for the ones that simply restate what was in the previous sentence. New sentences should contain new information and new insights into the subject of the text. If asked for the paragraph to which a sentence would most naturally be added, find a key noun or word in that new sentence. Then find the paragraph containing exactly or another word closely related to that key noun or word. That is the paragraph that should include the new sentence.

Some questions will ask what purpose a phrase fulfilled in a particular text. It depends upon the subject of the text. If the text is dramatic, then the phrase was probably used to show drama. If the text is comedic, then the phrase was probably to show comedy.

In related cases, you may be asked to provide a sentence that summarizes the text. Simple sentences, without wordy phrases, are usually best. If asked for a succinct answer, then the shorter the answer, the more likely it is correct.

Simplicity is Bliss

Simplicity cannot be overstated. You should never choose a longer, more complicated, or wordier replacement if a simple one will do. When a point can be made with fewer words, choose that answer. However, never sacrifice the flow of text for simplicity. If an answer is simple, but does not make sense, then it is not correct.

Beware of added phrases that don't add anything of meaning, such as "to be" or "as to them". Often these added phrases will occur just before a colon, which may come before a list of items. However, the colon does not need a lengthy introduction. The italics phrases in the below examples are wordy and unnecessary. They should be removed and the colon placed directly after the words "sport" and "following".

Example 1: There are many advantages to running as a sport, of which the top advantages are:

Example 2: The school supplies necessary were the following, of which a few are:

Parallelism

Often clues to the best answer are given within the text, if you know where to look for them. The correct answer will always be parallel in grammar type, punctuation, format, and tense as the rest of the sentence.

Grammar Type

If a series of nouns is given, then make sure your choice is a noun. If those nouns are plural, then ensure that your choice is plural.

Example: schools, politics, and governments

If a series of verbs is given, then make sure your choice is a verb.
Example: eat, sleep, and drink

If a series of infinitives is given, then make sure your choice is an infinitive.
Example: to trust, to honor, and to obey

If a series of phrases is given, then make sure your choice is a similar phrase.
Example: of controlling, of policing, and of maintaining

Punctuation

If a section of text has an opening dash, parentheses, or comma at the beginning of a phrase, then you can be sure there should be a matching closing dash, parentheses, or comma at the end of the phrase. If items in a series all have commas between them, then any additional items in that series will also gain commas. Do not alternate punctuation. If a dash is at the beginning of a statement, then do not put a parenthesis at the ending of the statement.

Tense

Items in a series will also have the same tense.
If past tense is being used for the other items in the series, then maintain the same past tense for your response.

Example: sailed, flew, and raced

If present participle tense is being used for the other items in the series, then maintain the same present participle tense for your response.
Example: sailing, flying, and racing

In order to test the tense of a verb, you can put it into a sentence that includes yourself. I sailed the boat. I flew the plane. I raced the car. These all fit into similar sentence structures and are in fact the same tense.

Added phrases

Any sentence or phrase added to a paragraph must maintain the same train of thought. This is particularly true when the word "and" is used. The word "and" joins two comments of like nature.

Example: These men were tough. They were accustomed to a hard life, and could watch a man die without blinking.

If an added phrase does not maintain a consistent train of thought, it will be set out with a word such as "but", "however", or "although". The new phrase would then be inconsistent to the train of thought and would offer a contrast.

Example: These men were tough. They were accustomed to a hard life, but to watch a man die would cause them to faint.

A tough man accustomed to a hard life is not expected to faint. Therefore the statements are contrasting and must have a contrasting transitional word, such as "but."

Word Confusion

Contractions

All contractions, such as they're, it's, and who's are actually two words joined together by the use of an apostrophe to replace a missing letter or letters. Whenever a contraction is encountered, it can be broken down into the two distinct words that make it up.

Example: I wouldn't eat in the cafeteria. = I would not eat in the cafeteria.

The apostrophe in the contraction is always located where the missing letter or letters should be. In the examples below, the apostrophe replaces the "o" in the word "not". The contraction "doesn't" actually stands for the two words "does not".

Incorrect Example: He does'nt live here.
Correct Example: He doesn't live here.

Whenever there is a contraction in an answer choice, it can always be replaced by the two words that make the contraction up. If necessary, scratch through the contractions in the choices, and replace them with the two words that make up the contraction. Otherwise the choices may be confusing. Alternatively, while reading the answer choices to yourself, instead of reading the contractions as a contraction, read them as the two separate words that make them up. Some contractions are especially confusing.

Its/It's

"It's" is actually a contraction for the two words "it is". Never confuse "it's" for the possessive pronoun "its". "It's" should only be used when the two words "it is" would make sense as a replacement. Use "its" in all other cases.

Example 1: It's going to rain later today. = It is going to rain later today.
Example 2: The dog chewed through its rope and ran away.

They're/Their/There

"They're" is actually a contraction for "they are", and those two words should always be used to replace "they're" when it is encountered.

Example: They're going to the movie with us. = They are going to the movie with us.

"Their" is an adjective used to show ownership.

Example 1: Their car is a red convertible.

Example 2: The students from each school sat in their own stands.

"There" should be used in all other cases.

Example 1: There exists an answer to every question.

Example 2: The man was over there.

Who's/Whose

Who's is actually a contraction for "who is", and those two words should always be used to replace who's when it is encountered.

Example: Who's going with me? = Who is going with me?

Whose would be used in all other cases, where "who is" does not fit.

Example: Whose car is this?

Their/His

"Their" is a plural possessive pronoun, referring to multiple people or objects.

Example: The men went to their cars.

"His" is a singular possessive, referring to an individual person or object.

Example: The man went to his car.

Which/That/Who

"Which" should be used to refer to things only.

John's dog, which was called Max, is large and fierce.

"That" may be used to refer to either persons or things.

Is this the only book that Louis L'Amour wrote?

Is Louis L'Amour the author that [or who] wrote Western novels?

"Who" should be used to refer to persons only.

Mozart was the composer who [or that] wrote those operas.

Who/Whom or Whoever/Whomever

Who/whom will be encountered in two forms, as an interrogative pronoun in a question, or as a relative pronoun not in a question.

1. Interrogative pronoun in a question. If the answer to the question would include the pronouns he, she, we, or they, then "who" is correct.

Example: Who threw the ball? He threw the ball.

If the answer to the question would include the pronouns him, her, us, or them, then "whom" is correct.

Example: With whom did you play baseball? I played baseball with him.

2. Relative pronoun NOT in a question.

If who/whom is followed by a verb, typically use "who".

Example: Peter Jackson was an obscure director who became a celebrity overnight.

If who/whom is followed by a noun, typically use "whom".

Example: Bob, whom we follow throughout his career, rose swiftly up the ladder of success.

However, beware of the insertion of phrases or expressions immediately following the use of who/whom. Sometimes, the phrase can be skipped without the sentence losing its meaning.

Example: This is the woman who, we believe, will win the race.

To determine the proper selection of who/whom, skip the phrase "we believe". Thus, "who" would come before "will win", a verb, making the choice of "who" correct.

In other cases, the sentence should be rephrased in order to make the right decision.

Example: I can't remember who the author of "War and Peace" is.
To determine the proper selection of who/whom, rephrase the sentence to state, "I can't remember who is the author of 'War and Peace'."

Correct pronoun usage in combinations

To determine the correct pronoun form in a compound subject, try each subject separately with the verb, adapting the form as necessary. Your ear will tell you which form is correct.

Example: Bob and (I, me) will be going.
Restate the sentence twice, using each subject individually. Bob will be going. I will be going.
"Me will be going" does not make sense.

When a pronoun is used with a noun immediately following (as in "we boys"), say the sentence without the added noun. Your ear will tell you the correct pronoun form.

Example: (We/Us) boys played football last year.
Restate the sentence twice, without the noun. We played football last year. Us played football last year. Clearly "We played football last year" makes more sense.

Commas

Flow

Commas break the flow of text. To test whether they are necessary, while reading the text to yourself, pause for a moment at each comma. If the pauses seem natural, then the commas are correct. If they are not, then the commas are not correct.

Nonessential clauses and phrases

A comma should be used to set off nonessential clauses and nonessential participial phrases from the rest of the sentence. To determine if a clause is essential, remove it from the sentence. If the removal of the clause would alter the meaning of the sentence, then it is essential. Otherwise, it is nonessential.

Example: John Smith, who was a disciple of Andrew Collins, was a noted archeologist.

In the example above, the sentence describes John Smith's fame in archeology. The fact that he was a disciple of Andrew Collins is not necessary to that meaning. Therefore, separating it from the rest of the sentence with commas, is correct.

Do not use a comma if the clause or phrase is essential to the meaning of the sentence.

Example: Anyone who appreciates obscure French poetry will enjoy reading the book.

If the phrase "who appreciates obscure French poetry" is removed, the sentence would indicate that anyone would enjoy reading the book, not just those with an appreciation for obscure French poetry. However, the sentence implies that the book's enjoyment may not be for everyone, so the phrase is essential.

Another perhaps easier way to determine if the clause is essential is to see if it has a comma at its beginning or end. Consistent, parallel punctuation must be used, and so if you can determine a comma exists at one side of the clause, then you can be certain that a comma should exist on the opposite side.

Subjects and verbs

Subjects and verbs must not be separated by commas. However, a pair of commas setting off a nonessential phrase is allowed.

Example: The office, which closed today for the festival, was open on Thursday. "Was" is the verb, while "office" is the subject. The comma pair between them sets off a nonessential phrase, "which is allowed". A single comma between them would not be allowed.

If you are trying to find the subject, first find the verb and use it to fill in the blank in the following sentence. Who or what ____?

Example: The boy on the bicycle raced down the hill.
The verb is "raced". If you can find "raced" and identify it as the verb, ask yourself, "Who or what raced down the hill?" The answer to that question is the subject, in this case "boy".

Independent clauses

Use a comma before the words and, but, or, nor, for, yet when they join independent clauses. To determine if two clauses are independent, remove the word that joins them. If the two clauses are capable of being their own sentence by themselves, then they are independent and need a comma between them.

Example: He ran down the street, and then he ran over the bridge.
He ran down the street. Then he ran over the bridge. These are both clauses capable of being their own sentence. Therefore a comma must be used along with the word "and" to join the two clauses together.

If one or more of the clauses would be a fragment if left alone, then it must be joined to another clause and does not need a comma between them.

Example: He ran down the street and over the bridge.
He ran down the street. Over the bridge. "Over the bridge" is a sentence fragment and is not capable of existing on its own. No comma is necessary to join it with "He ran down the street".

Note that this does not cover the use of "and" when separating items in a series, such as "red, white, and blue". In these cases a comma is not always necessary between the last two items in the series, but in general it is best to use one.

Parenthetical expressions

Commas should separate parenthetical expressions such as the following: after all, by the way, for example, in fact, on the other hand.
Example: By the way, she is in my biology class.

If the parenthetical expression is in the middle of the sentence, a comma would be both before and after it.
Example: She is, after all, in my biology class.

However, these expressions are not always used parenthetically. In these cases, commas are not used. To determine if an expression is parenthetical, see if it would need a pause if you were reading the text. If it does, then it is parenthetical and needs commas.

Example: You can tell by the way she plays the violin that she enjoys its music.
No pause is necessary in reading that example sentence. Therefore the phrase "by the way" does not need commas around it.

Sentence beginnings

Use a comma after words such as so, well, yes, no, and why when they begin a sentence.

Example 1: So, you were there when they visited.

Example 2: Well, I really haven't thought about it.

Example 3: Yes, I heard your question.

Example 4: No, I don't think I'll go to the movie.

Example 5: Why, I can't imagine where I left my keys.

Hyphens

Hyphenate a compound adjective that is directly before the noun it describes.

Example 1: He was the best-known kid in the school.

Example 2: The shot came from that grass-covered hill.

Example 3: The well-drained fields were dry soon after the rain.

Semicolons

Period replacement

A semicolon is often described as either a weak period or strong comma. Semicolons should separate independent clauses that could stand alone as separate sentences. To test where a semicolon should go, replace it with a period in your mind. If the two independent clauses would seem normal with the period, then the semicolon is in the right place.

Example: The rain had finally stopped; a few rays of sunshine were pushing their way through the clouds.

The rain had finally stopped. A few rays of sunshine were pushing their way through the clouds. These two sentences can exist independently with a period between them. Because they are also closely related in thought, a semicolon is a good choice to combine them.

Related/Unrelated

A semicolon should only join clauses that are closely related in thought.

Example: The lasagna is delicious; I'll have another piece.

In this example, the two clauses are closely related in thought; a semicolon should join them.

Do not use a semicolon if the clauses are unrelated in thought.

Example: For Steve, oil painting was a difficult medium to master. He had enjoyed taking photographs when he was younger.

In this example, the two sentences would be unrelated clauses, so a semicolon should not join them.

Comparative methods of joining clauses

Use a semicolon between independent clauses not joined by "and, but, for, or, nor, yet, so, since, therefore". Semicolons should rarely be next to these words, but is rather used in place of a comma and these words.

Example 1: He had the gun; it hung from a holster at his side.

In the example above, no "and" or comma is necessary.

Example 2: He had the gun, and it hung from a holster at his side.

In the example above, the comma combined with the word "and" help to join the two independent clauses.

Transitions

When a semicolon is next to a transition word, such as "however", it comes before the word.

Example: The man in the red shirt stood next to her; however, he did not know her name.

If these two clauses were separated with a period, the period would go before the word "however" creating the following two sentences: The man in the red shirt stood next to her. However, he did not know her name. The semicolon can function as a weak period and join the two clauses by replacing the period.

Items in a series

Semicolons are used to separate 3 or more items in a series that have a comma internally.

Example: The club president appointed the following to chair the various committees: John Smith, planning; Jessica Graham, membership; Paul Randolph, financial; and Jerry Short, legal.

Parentheses

Years

Parentheses should be used around years.

Example: The presidency of Franklin Delano Roosevelt (1932-1945) was the longest one in American history.

Nonessential information

Parentheses can be used around information that is added to a sentence but is not essential. Commas or dashes could also be used around these nonessential phrases.

Example: George Eliot (whose real name was Mary Ann Evans) wrote poems and several well-known novels.

Colon

Items in a series

A colon should precede a list of items in which you could logically insert the word "namely" after it.

Example: The syllabus stated that each student would need the following: a sketch pad, a set of paint brushes, an easel, a pencil, and a box of crayons.

If the word namely were inserted, the example sentence would read, "The syllabus stated that each student would need the following: "namely" a sketch pad, a set of paint brushes, an easel, a pencil, and a box of crayons." Because the sentence still flows with the word "namely" inserted, a colon is necessary.

When the list immediately follows a verb or preposition, do not use a colon.

Example 1: The emergency kit included safety flares, jumper cables, and a flashlight.
Example 2: Each student taking the test was provided with two sharpened pencils, paper, a calculator, and a ruler.
Note that the insertion of the word "namely" would be awkward in the above two examples.

Independent clauses

Use a colon between independent clauses when the second clause explains or restates the idea of the first.
Example: Benjamin Franklin had many talents: he was an inventor, a writer, a politician, and a philosopher.

Apostrophes

If the noun is plural and ends in an "s", the possessive apostrophe would come after the word, without the addition of another "s".
Example: The students' hats were wet from the rain.
In the example above, there are plural or many students, all of whom have wet hats.

If the noun is plural and does not end in an "s", the possessive apostrophe would come after the word, with the addition of an "s".
Example: The mice's feet were wet from the rain.

If the noun is singular, the possessive apostrophe is followed by an "s".

Example: The student's hat was wet from the rain.

In the example above, there is only one student, whose hat is wet.

The Math Test

Numbers and their Classifications

Numbers are the basic building blocks of mathematics. Specific features of numbers are identified by the following terms:

Integers – The set of whole positive and negative numbers, including zero. Integers do not include fractions ($\frac{1}{3}$), decimals (0.56), or mixed numbers ($7\frac{3}{4}$).

Prime number – A whole number greater than 1 that has only two factors, itself and 1; that is, a number that can be divided evenly only by 1 and itself.

Composite number – A whole number greater than 1 that has more than two different factors; in other words, any whole number that is not a prime number. For example: The composite number 8 has the factors of 1, 2, 4, and 8.

Even number – Any integer that can be divided by 2 without leaving a remainder. For example: 2, 4, 6, 8, and so on.

Odd number – Any integer that cannot be divided evenly by 2. For example: 3, 5, 7, 9, and so on.

Decimal number – a number that uses a decimal point to show the part of the number that is less than one. Example: 1.234.

Decimal point – a symbol used to separate the ones place from the tenths place in decimals or dollars from cents in currency.

Decimal place – the position of a number to the right of the decimal point. In the decimal 0.123, the 1 is in the first place to the right of the decimal point, indicating tenths; the 2 is in the second place, indicating hundredths; and the 3 is in the third place, indicating thousandths.

The decimal, or base 10, system is a number system that uses ten different digits (0, 1, 2, 3, 4, 5, 6, 7, 8, 9). An example of a number system that uses something other than ten digits is the binary, or base 2, number system, used by computers, which uses only the numbers 0 and 1. It is thought that the decimal system originated because people had only their 10 fingers for counting.

Rational, irrational, and real numbers can be described as follows:

Rational numbers include all integers, decimals, and fractions. Any terminating or repeating decimal number is a rational number.

Irrational numbers cannot be written as fractions or decimals because the number of decimal places is infinite and there is no recurring pattern of digits within the number. For example, pi (π) begins with 3.141592 and continues without terminating or repeating, so pi is an irrational number.

Real numbers are the set of all rational and irrational numbers.

Operations

There are four basic mathematical operations:

Addition increases the value of one quantity by the value of another quantity. Example: $2 + 4 = 6$; $8 + 9 = 17$. The result is called the sum. With addition, the order does not matter. $4 + 2 = 2 + 4$.

Subtraction is the opposite operation to addition; it decreases the value of one quantity by the value of another quantity. Example: $6 - 4 = 2$; $17 - 8 = 9$. The result is called the difference. Note that with subtraction, the order does matter. $6 - 4 \neq 4 - 6$.

Multiplication can be thought of as repeated addition. One number tells how many times to add the other number to itself. Example: 3×2 (three times two) $= 2 + 2 + 2 = 6$. With multiplication, the order does not matter. $2 \times 3 = 3 \times 2$ or $3 + 3 = 2 + 2 + 2$.

Division is the opposite operation to multiplication; one number tells us how many parts to divide the other number into. Example: $20 \div 4 = 5$; if 20 is split into 4 equal parts, each part is 5. With division, the order of the numbers does matter. $20 \div 4 \neq 4 \div 20$.

An exponent is a superscript number placed next to another number at the top right. It indicates how many times the base number is to be multiplied by itself. Exponents provide a shorthand way to write what would be a longer mathematical expression. Example: $a^2 = a \times a$; $2^4 = 2 \times 2 \times 2 \times 2$. A number with an exponent of 2 is said to be "squared," while a number with an exponent of 3 is said to be "cubed." The value of a number raised to an exponent is called its power. So, 8^4 is read as "8 to the 4th power," or "8 raised to the power of 4." A negative exponent is the same as the reciprocal of a positive exponent. Example: $a^{-2} = \frac{1}{a^2}$.

Parentheses are used to designate which operations should be done first when there are multiple operations. Example: $4 - (2 + 1) = 1$; the parentheses tell us that we must add 2 and 1, and then subtract the sum from 4, rather than subtracting 2 from 4 and then adding 1 (this would give us an answer of 3).

Order of Operations is a set of rules that dictates the order in which we must perform each operation in an expression so that we will evaluate at accurately. If we have an expression that includes multiple different operations, Order of Operations tells us which operations to do first. The most common mnemonic for Order of Operations is PEMDAS, or "Please Excuse My Dear Aunt Sally." PEMDAS stands for Parentheses, Exponents, Multiplication, Division, Addition, Subtraction. It is important to understand that multiplication and division have equal precedence, as do addition and subtraction, so those pairs of operations are simply worked from left to right in order.

Example: Evaluate the expression $5 + 20 \div 4 \times (2 + 3)^2 - 6$ using the correct order of operations.

P: Perform the operations inside the parentheses, $(2 + 3) = 5$.

E: Simplify the exponents, $(5)^2 = 25$.

The equation now looks like this: $5 + 20 \div 4 \times 25 - 6$.

MD: Perform multiplication and division from left to right, $20 \div 4 = 5$; then $5 \times 25 = 125$.

The equation now looks like this: $5 + 125 - 6$.

AS: Perform addition and subtraction from left to right, $5 + 125 = 130$; then $130 - 6 = 124$.

The laws of exponents are as follows:

1) Any number to the power of 1 is equal to itself: $a^1 = a$.

2) The number 1 raised to any power is equal to 1: $1^n = 1$.

3) Any number raised to the power of 0 is equal to 1: $a^0 = 1$.

4) Add exponents to multiply powers of the same base number: $a^n \times a^m = a^{n+m}$.

5) Subtract exponents to divide powers of the same number; that is $a^n \div a^m = a^{n-m}$.

6) Multiply exponents to raise a power to a power: $(a^n)^m = a^{n \times m}$.

7) If multiplied or divided numbers inside parentheses are collectively raised to a power, this is the same as each individual term being raised to that power: $(a \times b)^n = a^n \times b^n$; $(a \div b)^n = a^n \div b^n$.

Note: Exponents do not have to be integers. Fractional or decimal exponents follow all the rules above as well. Example: $5^{\frac{1}{4}} \times 5^{\frac{3}{4}} = 5^{\frac{1}{4}+\frac{3}{4}} = 5^1 = 5$.

A root, such as a square root, is another way of writing a fractional exponent. Instead of using a superscript, roots use the radical symbol ($\sqrt{}$) to indicate the operation. A radical will have a number underneath the bar, and may sometimes have a number in the upper left: $\sqrt[n]{a}$, read as "the nth root of a." The relationship between radical notation and exponent notation can be described by this equation: $\sqrt[n]{a} = a^{\frac{1}{n}}$. The two special cases of $n = 2$ and $n = 3$ are called square roots and cube roots. If there is no number to the upper left, it is understood to be a square root ($n = 2$). Nearly all of the roots you encounter will be square roots. A square root is the same as a number raised to the one-half power. When we say that a is the square root of b ($a = \sqrt{b}$), we mean that a multiplied by itself equals b: ($a \times a = b$).

A perfect square is a number that has an integer for its square root. There are 10 perfect squares from 1 to 100: 1, 4, 9, 16, 25, 36, 49, 64, 81, 100 (the squares of integers 1 through 10).

Scientific notation is a way of writing large numbers in a shorter form. The form $a \times 10^n$ is used in scientific notation, where a is greater than or equal to 1, but less than 10, and n is the number of places the decimal must move to get from the original number to a. Example: The number 230,400,000 is cumbersome to write. To write the value in scientific notation, place a decimal point between the first and second numbers, and include all digits through the last non-zero digit ($a = 2.304$). To find the appropriate power of 10, count the number of places the decimal point had to move ($n = 8$). The number is positive if the decimal moved to the left, and negative if it moved to the right. We can then write 230,400,000 as 2.304×10^8. If we look instead at the number 0.00002304, we have the same value for a, but this time the decimal moved 5 places to the right ($n = -5$). Thus, 0.00002304 can be written as 2.304×10^{-5}. Using this notation makes it simple to compare very large or very small numbers. By comparing exponents, it is easy to see that 3.28×10^4 is smaller than 1.51×10^5, because 4 is less than 5.

Factors and Multiples

Factors are numbers that are multiplied together to obtain a product. For example, in the equation $2 \times 3 = 6$, the numbers 2 and 3 are factors. A prime number has only two factors (1 and itself), but other numbers can have many factors.
A common factor is a number that divides exactly into two or more other numbers. For example, the factors of 12 are 1, 2, 3, 4, 6, and 12, while the factors of 15 are 1, 3, 5, and 15. The common factors of 12 and 15 are 1 and 3.
A prime factor is also a prime number. Therefore, the prime factors of 12 are 1, 2, and 3. For 15, the prime factors are 1, 3, and 5.

The greatest common factor (GCF) is the largest number that is a factor of two or more numbers. For example, the factors of 15 are 1, 3, 5, and 15; the factors of 35 are 1, 5, 7, and 35. Therefore, the greatest common factor of 15 and 35 is 5. The least common multiple (LCM) is the smallest number that is a multiple of two or more numbers. For example, the multiples of 3 include 3, 6, 9, 12, 15, etc.; the multiples of 5 include 5, 10, 15, 20, etc. Therefore, the least common multiple of 3 and 5 is 15.

Fractions, Percentages, and Related Concepts

A fraction is a number that is expressed as one integer written above another integer, with a dividing line between them ($\frac{x}{y}$). It represents the quotient of the two numbers "x divided by y." It can also be thought of as x out of y equal parts. The top number of a fraction is called the numerator, and it represents the number of parts under consideration. The 1 in $\frac{1}{4}$ means that 1 part out of the whole is being considered in the calculation. The bottom number of a fraction is called the denominator, and it represents the total number of equal parts. The 4 in $\frac{1}{4}$ means that the whole consists of 4 equal parts. A fraction cannot have a denominator of zero; this is referred to as "undefined."

Fractions can be manipulated, without changing the value of the fraction, by multiplying or dividing (but not adding or subtracting) both the numerator and denominator by the same number. If you divide both numbers by a common factor, you are reducing or simplifying the fraction. Two fractions that have the same value, but are expressed differently are known as equivalent fractions. For example, $\frac{2}{10}, \frac{3}{15}, \frac{4}{20}$, and $\frac{5}{25}$ are all equivalent fractions. They can also all be reduced or simplified to $\frac{1}{5}$.

When two fractions are manipulated so that they have the same denominator, this is known as finding a common denominator. The number chosen to be that common denominator should be the least common multiple of the two original denominators. Example: $\frac{3}{4}$ and $\frac{5}{6}$; the least common multiple of 4 and 6 is 12. Manipulating to achieve the common denominator: $\frac{3}{4} = \frac{9}{12}$; $\frac{5}{6} = \frac{10}{12}$.

If two fractions have a common denominator, they can be added or subtracted simply by adding or subtracting the two numerators and retaining the same denominator. Example: $\frac{1}{2} + \frac{1}{4} = \frac{2}{4} + \frac{1}{4} = \frac{3}{4}$. If the two fractions do not already have the same denominator, one or both of them must be manipulated to achieve a common denominator before they can be added or subtracted.

Two fractions can be multiplied by multiplying the two numerators to find the new numerator and the two denominators to find the new denominator. Example: $\frac{1}{3} \times \frac{2}{3} = \frac{1 \times 2}{3 \times 3} = \frac{2}{9}$.

Two fractions can be divided flipping the numerator and denominator of the second fraction and then proceeding as though it were a multiplication. Example: $\frac{2}{3} \div \frac{3}{4} = \frac{2}{3} \times \frac{4}{3} = \frac{8}{9}$.

A fraction whose denominator is greater than its numerator is known as a proper fraction, while a fraction whose numerator is greater than its denominator is known as an improper fraction. Proper fractions have values less than one and improper fractions have values greater than one.

A mixed number is a number that contains both an integer and a fraction. Any improper fraction can be rewritten as a mixed number. Example: $\frac{8}{3} = \frac{6}{3} + \frac{2}{3} = 2 + \frac{2}{3} = 2\frac{2}{3}$. Similarly, any mixed number can be rewritten as an improper fraction. Example: $1\frac{3}{5} = 1 + \frac{3}{5} = \frac{5}{5} + \frac{3}{5} = \frac{8}{5}$.

Percentages can be thought of as fractions that are based on a whole of 100; that is, one whole is equal to 100%. The word percent means "per hundred." Fractions can be expressed as percents by finding equivalent fractions with a denomination of 100. Example: $\frac{7}{10} = \frac{70}{100} = 70\%$; $\frac{1}{4} = \frac{25}{100} = 25\%$.

To express a percentage as a fraction, divide the percentage number by 100 and reduce the fraction to its simplest possible terms. Example: $60\% = \frac{60}{100} = \frac{3}{5}$; $96\% = \frac{96}{100} = \frac{24}{25}$.

Converting decimals to percentages and percentages to decimals is as simple as moving the decimal point. To convert from a decimal to a percent, move the decimal point two places to the right. To convert from a percent to a decimal, move it two places to the left. Example: 0.23 = 23%; 5.34 = 534%; 0.007 = 0.7%; 700% = 7.00; 86% = 0.86; 0.15% = 0.0015.

It may be helpful to remember that the percentage number will always be larger than the equivalent decimal number.

A percentage problem can be presented three main ways: (1) Find what percentage of some number another number is. Example: What percentage of 40 is 8? (2) Find what number is some percentage of a given number. Example: What number is 20% of 40? (3) Find what number another number is a given percentage of. Example: What number is 8 20% of? The three components in all of these cases are the same: a whole (W), a part (P), and a percentage (%). These are related by the equation: $P = W \times \%$. This is the form of the equation you would use to solve problems of type (2). To solve types (1) and (3), you would use these two forms: $\% = \frac{P}{W}$ and $W = \frac{P}{\%}$.

The thing that frequently makes percentage problems difficult is that they are most often also word problems, so a large part of solving them is figuring out which quantities are what. Example: In a school cafeteria, 7 students choose pizza, 9 choose hamburgers, and 4 choose tacos. Find the percentage that chooses tacos. To find the whole, you must first add all of the parts: 7 + 9 + 4 = 20. The percentage can then be found by dividing the part by the whole ($\% = \frac{P}{W}$): $\frac{4}{20} = \frac{20}{100} = 20\%$.

A ratio is a comparison of two quantities in a particular order. Example: If there are 14 computers in a lab, and the class has 20 students, there is a student to computer ratio of 20 to 14, commonly written as 20:14. Ratios are normally reduced to their smallest whole number representation, so 20:14 would be reduced to 10:7 by dividing both sides by 2.

A proportion is a relationship between two quantities that dictates how one changes when the other changes. A direct proportion describes a relationship in which a quantity increases by a set amount for every increase in the other quantity, or decreases by that same amount for every decrease in the other quantity. Example: Assuming a constant driving speed, the time required for a car trip increases as the distance of the trip increases. The distance to be traveled and the time required to travel are directly proportional.

Inverse proportion is a relationship in which an increase in one quantity is accompanied by a decrease in the other, or vice versa. Example: the time required for a car trip decreases as the speed increases, and increases as the speed decreases, so the time required is inversely proportional to the speed of the car.

Triangles

Rules

The Triangle Inequality Theorem states that the sum of the measures of any two sides of a triangle is always greater than the measure of the third side. If the sum of the measures of two sides were equal to the third side, a triangle would be impossible because the two sides would lie flat across the third side and there would be no vertex. If the sum of the measures of two of the sides was less than the third side, a closed figure would be impossible because the two shortest sides would never meet.

The sum of the measures of the interior angles of a triangle is always 180°. Therefore, a triangle can never have more than one angle greater than or equal to 90°.

In any triangle, the angles opposite congruent sides are congruent, and the sides opposite congruent angles are congruent. The largest angle is always opposite the longest side, and the smallest angle is always opposite the shortest side.

The line segment that joins the midpoints of any two sides of a triangle is always parallel to the third side and exactly half the length of the third side.

Area and perimeter formulas

The perimeter of any triangle is found by summing the three side lengths; $P = a + b + c$. For an equilateral triangle, this is the same as $P = 3s$, where s is any side length, since all three sides are the same length.

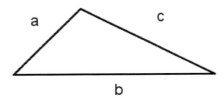

The area of any triangle can be found by taking half the product of one side length (base or b) and the perpendicular distance from that side to the opposite vertex (height or h). In equation form, $A = \frac{1}{2}bh$. For many triangles, it may be difficult to calculate h, so using one of the other formulas given here may be easier.

Another formula that works for any triangle is $A = \sqrt{s(s-a)(s-b)(s-c)}$, where A is the area, s is the semiperimeter $s = \frac{a+b+c}{2}$, and a, b, and c are the lengths of the three sides.

The area of an equilateral triangle can found by the formula $A = \frac{\sqrt{3}}{4}s^2$, where A is the area and s is the length of a side. You could use the $30° - 60° - 90°$ ratios to find the height of the triangle and then use the standard triangle area formula, but this is faster.

The area of an isosceles triangle can found by the formula, $A = \frac{1}{2}b\sqrt{a^2 - \frac{b^2}{4}}$, where A is the area, b is the base (the unique side), and a is the length of one of the two congruent sides. If you do not remember this formula, you can use the Pythagorean Theorem to find the height so you can use the standard formula for the area of a triangle.

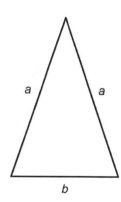

Quadrilaterals

Area and perimeter formulas

The area of a square is found by using the formula $A = s^2$, where and s is the length of one side.

The perimeter of a square is found by using the formula $P = 4s$, where s is the length of one side. Because all four sides are equal in a square, it is faster to multiply the length of one side by 4 than to add the same number four times. You could use the formulas for rectangles and get the same answer.

The area of a rectangle is found by the formula $A = lw$, where A is the area of the rectangle, l is the length (usually considered to be the longer side) and w is the width (usually considered to be the shorter side). The numbers for l and w are interchangeable.

The perimeter of a rectangle is found by the formula $P = 2l + 2w$ or $P = 2(l + w)$, where l is the length, and w is the width. It may be easier to add the length and width first and then double the result, as in the second formula.

The area of a parallelogram is found by the formula $A = bh$, where b is the length of the base, and h is the height. Note that the base and height correspond to the length and width in a rectangle, so this formula would apply to rectangles as well. Do not confuse the height of a parallelogram with the length of the second side. The two are only the same measure in the case of a rectangle.

The perimeter of a parallelogram is found by the formula $P = 2a + 2b$ or $P = 2(a + b)$, where a and b are the lengths of the two sides.

The area of a trapezoid is found by the formula $A = \frac{1}{2}h(b_1 + b_2)$, where h is the height (segment joining and perpendicular to the parallel bases), and b_1 and b_2 are the two parallel sides (bases). Do not use one of the other two sides as the height unless that side is also perpendicular to the parallel bases.

The perimeter of a trapezoid is found by the formula $P = a + b_1 + c + b_2$, where a, b_1, c, and b_2 are the four sides of the trapezoid.

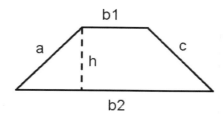

Polynomial Algebra

Equations are made up of monomials and polynomials. A *Monomial* is a single variable or product of constants and variables, such as x, $2x$, or $\frac{2}{x}$. There will never be addition or subtraction symbols in a monomial. Like monomials have like variables, but they may have different coefficients. *Polynomials* are algebraic expressions which use addition and subtraction to combine two or more monomials. Two terms make a binomial; three terms make a trinomial; etc.. The *Degree of a Monomial* is the sum of the exponents of the variables. The *Degree of a Polynomial* is the highest degree of any individual term.

To multiply two binomials, follow the *FOIL* method. FOIL stands for:
- First: Multiply the first term of each binomial
- Outer: Multiply the outer terms of each binomial
- Inner: Multiply the inner terms of each binomial
- Last: Multiply the last term of each binomial

Using FOIL, $(Ax + By)(Cx + Dy) = ACx^2 + ADxy + BCxy + BDy^2$.

To divide polynomials, begin by arranging the terms of each polynomial in order of one variable. You may arrange in ascending or descending order, but be consistent with both polynomials. To get the first term of the quotient, divide the first term of the dividend by the first term of the divisor. Multiply the first term of the quotient by the entire divisor and subtract that product from the dividend. Repeat for the second and successive terms until you either get a remainder of zero or a remainder whose degree is less than the degree of the divisor. If the quotient has a remainder, write the answer as a mixed expression in the form: quotient $+ \frac{\text{remainder}}{\text{divisor}}$.

Rational Expressions are fractions with polynomials in both the numerator and the denominator; the value of the polynomial in the denominator cannot be equal to zero. To add or subtract rational expressions, first find the common denominator, then rewrite each fraction as an equivalent fraction with the common denominator. Finally, add or subtract the numerators to get the numerator of the answer, and keep the common denominator as the denominator of the answer. When multiplying rational expressions factor each polynomial and cancel like factors (a factor which appears in both the numerator and the denominator). Then, multiply all remaining factors in the numerator to get the numerator of the product, and multiply the remaining factors in the denominator to get the denominator of the product. Remember – cancel entire factors, not individual terms. To divide rational expressions, take the reciprocal of the divisor (the rational expression you are dividing by) and multiply by the dividend.

Below are patterns of some special products to remember: *perfect trinomial squares*, the *difference between two squares*, the *sum and difference of two cubes*, and *perfect cubes*.

- Perfect Trinomial Squares: $x^2 + 2xy + y^2 = (x + y)^2$ or $x^2 - 2xy + y^2 = (x - y)^2$
- Difference Between Two Squares: $x^2 - y^2 = (x + y)(x - y)$

- Sum of Two Cubes: $x^3 + y^3 = (x + y)(x^2 - xy + y^2)$

  Note: the second factor is NOT the same as a perfect trinomial square, so do not try to factor it further.

- Difference Between Two Cubes: $x^3 - y^3 = (x - y)(x^2 + xy + y^2)$

  Again, the second factor is NOT the same as a perfect trinomial square.

- Perfect Cubes: $x^3 + 3x^2y + 3xy^2 + y^3 = (x + y)^3$ and $x^3 - 3x^2y + 3xy^2 - y^3 = (x - y)^3$

In order to *factor* a polynomial, first check for a common monomial factor. When the greatest common monomial factor has been factored out, look for patterns of special products: differences of two squares, the sum or difference of two cubes for binomial factors, or perfect trinomial squares for trinomial factors. If the factor is a trinomial but not a perfect trinomial square, look for a factorable form, such as $x^2 + (a + b)x + ab = (x + a)(x + b)$ or $(ac)x^2 + (ad + bc)x + bd = (ax + b)(cx + d)$. For factors with four terms, look for groups to factor. Once you have found the factors, write the original polynomial as the product of all the factors. Make sure all of the polynomial factors are prime. Monomial factors may be prime or composite. Check your work by multiplying the factors to make sure you get the original polynomial.

Solving Quadratic Equations

The *Quadratic Formula* is used to solve quadratic equations when other methods are more difficult. To use the quadratic formula to solve a quadratic equation, begin by rewriting the equation in standard form $ax^2 + bx + c = 0$, where a, b, and c are coefficients. Once you have identified the values of the coefficients, substitute those values into the quadratic formula $= \frac{-b \pm \sqrt{b^2 - 4ac}}{2a}$. Evaluate the equation and simplify the expression. Again, check each root by substituting into the original equation. In the quadratic formula, the portion of the formula under the radical ($b^2 - 4ac$) is called the *Discriminant*. If the discriminant is zero, there is only one root: zero. If the discriminant is positive, there are two different real roots. If the discriminant is negative, there are no real roots.

To solve a quadratic equation by *Factoring*, begin by rewriting the equation in standard form, if necessary. Factor the side with the variable then set each of the factors equal to zero and solve the resulting linear equations. Check your answers by substituting the roots you found into the original equation. If, when writing the equation in standard form, you have an equation in the form $x^2 + c = 0$ or $x^2 - c = 0$, set $x^2 = -c$ or $x^2 = c$ and take the square root of c. If $c = 0$, the only real root is zero. If c is positive, there are two real roots—the positive and negative square root values. If c is negative, there are no real roots because you cannot take the square root of a negative number.

To solve a quadratic equation by *Completing the Square*, rewrite the equation so that all terms containing the variable are on the left side of the equal sign, and all the constants are on the right side of the equal sign. Make sure the coefficient of the squared term is 1. If there is a coefficient with the squared term, divide each term on both sides of the equal side by that number. Next, work with the coefficient of the single-variable term. Square half of this coefficient, and add that value to both sides. Now you can factor the left side (the side containing the variable) as the square of a binomial. $x^2 + 2ax + a^2 = C \Rightarrow (x + a)^2 = C$, where x is the variable, and a and C are constants. Take the square root of both sides and solve for the variable. Substitute the value of the variable in the original problem to check your work.

Statistics

Statistics is the branch of mathematics that deals with collecting, recording, interpreting, illustrating, and analyzing large amounts of data. The following terms are often used in the discussion of data and statistics:

Data – the collective name for pieces of information (singular is datum).

Quantitative data – measurements (such as length, mass, and speed) that provide information about quantities in numbers

Qualitative data – information (such as colors, scents, tastes, and shapes) that cannot be measured using numbers

Discrete data – information that can be expressed only by a specific value, such as whole or half numbers; For example, since people can be counted only in whole numbers, a population count would be discrete data.

Continuous data – information (such as time and temperature) that can be expressed by any value within a given range

Primary data – information that has been collected directly from a survey, investigation, or experiment, such as a questionnaire or the recording of daily temperatures; Primary data that has not yet been organized or analyzed is called raw data.

Secondary data – information that has been collected, sorted, and processed by the researcher

Ordinal data – information that can be placed in numerical order, such as age or weight

Nominal data – information that cannot be placed in numerical order, such as names or places

Measures of Central Tendency

The quantities of mean, median, and mode are all referred to as measures of central tendency. They can each give a picture of what the whole set of data looks like with just a single number. Knowing what each of these values represents is vital to making use of the information they provide.

The mean, also known as the arithmetic mean or average, of a data set is calculated by summing all of the values in the set and dividing that sum by the number of values. For example, if a data set has 6 numbers and the sum of those 6 numbers is 30, the mean is calculated as 30/6 = 5.

The median is the middle value of a data set. The median can be found by putting the data set in numerical order, and locating the middle value. In the data set (1, 2, 3, 4, 5), the median is 3. If there is an even number of values in the set, the median is calculated by taking the average of the two middle values. In the data set, (1, 2, 3, 4, 5, 6), the median would be (3 + 4)/2 = 3.5.

The mode is the value that appears most frequently in the data set. In the data set (1, 2, 3, 4, 5, 5, 5), the mode would be 5 since the value 5 appears three times. If multiple values appear the same number of times, there are multiple values for the mode. If the data set were (1, 2, 2, 3, 4, 4, 5, 5), the modes would be 2, 4, and 5. If no value appears more than any other value in the data set, then there is no mode.

Measures of Dispersion

The standard deviation expresses how spread out the values of a distribution are from the mean. Standard deviation is given in the same units as the original data and is represented by a lower case sigma (σ).

A high standard deviation means that the values are very spread out. A low standard deviation means that the values are close together.

If every value in a distribution is increased or decreased by the same amount, the mean, median, and mode are increased or decreased by that amount, but the standard deviation stays the same.

If every value in a distribution is multiplied or divided by the same number, the mean, median, mode, and standard deviation will all be multiplied or divided by that number.

The range of a distribution is the difference between the highest and lowest values in the distribution. For example, in the data set (1, 3, 5, 7, 9, 11), the highest and lowest values are 11 and 1, respectively. The range then would be calculated as 11 – 1 = 10.

The three quartiles are the three values that divide a data set into four equal parts. Quartiles are generally only calculated for data sets with a large number of values. As a simple example, for the data set consisting of the numbers 1 through 99, the first quartile (Q1) would be 25, the second quartile (Q2), always equal to the median, would be 50, and the third quartile (Q3) would be 75. The difference between Q1 and Q3 is known as the interquartile range.

Probability

Probability is a branch of statistics that deals with the likelihood of something taking place. One classic example is a coin toss. There are only two possible results: heads or tails. The likelihood, or probability, that the coin will land as heads is 1 out of 2 (1/2, 0.5, 50%). Tails has the same probability. Another common example is a 6-sided die roll. There are six possible results from rolling a single die, each with an equal chance of happening, so the probability of any given number coming up is 1 out of 6.

Terms frequently used in probability:

Event – a situation that produces results of some sort (a coin toss)

Compound event – event that involves two or more items (rolling a pair of dice; taking the sum)

Outcome – a possible result in an experiment or event (heads, tails)

Desired outcome (or success) – an outcome that meets a particular set of criteria (a roll of 1 or 2 if we are looking for numbers less than 3)

Independent events – two or more events whose outcomes do not affect one another (two coins tossed at the same time)

Dependent events – two or more events whose outcomes affect one another (two cards drawn consecutively from the same deck)

Certain outcome – probability of outcome is 100% or 1

Impossible outcome – probability of outcome is 0% or 0

Mutually exclusive outcomes – two or more outcomes whose criteria cannot all be satisfied in a single event (a coin coming up heads and tails on the same toss)

Probability is the likelihood of a certain outcome occurring for a given event. The **theoretical probability** can usually be determined without actually performing the event. The likelihood of a outcome occurring, or the probability of an outcome occurring, is given by the formula

$$P(A) = \frac{\text{Number of acceptable outcomes}}{\text{Total number of possible outcomes}}$$

where $P(A)$ is the probability of an outcome A occurring, and each outcome is just as likely to occur as any other outcome. If each outcome has the same probability of occurring as every other possible outcome, the outcomes are said to be equally likely to occur. The total number of acceptable outcomes must be less than or equal to the total number of possible outcomes. If the two are equal, then the outcome is certain to occur and the probability is 1. If the number of acceptable outcomes is zero, then the outcome is impossible and the probability is 0.

Example:

There are 20 marbles in a bag and 5 are red. The theoretical probability of randomly selecting a red marble is 5 out of 20, (5/20 = 1/4, 0.25, or 25%).

When trying to calculate the probability of an event using the (desired outcomes)/(total outcomes formula), you may frequently find that there are too many outcomes to individually count them. Permutation and combination formulas offer a shortcut to counting outcomes. The primary distinction between permutations and combinations is that permutations take into account order, while combinations do not. To calculate the number of possible groupings, there are two necessary parameters: the number of items available for selection and the number to be selected. The number of **permutations** of r items given a set of n items can be calculated as $_nP_r = \frac{n!}{(n-r)!}$. The number of **combinations** of r items given a set of n items can be calculated as $_nC_r = \frac{n!}{r!(n-r)!}$ or $_nC_r = \frac{_nP_r}{r!}$.

Example: Suppose you want to calculate how many different 5-card hands can be drawn from a deck of 52 cards. This is a combination since the order of the cards in a hand does not matter. There are 52 cards available, and 5 to be selected. Thus, the number of different hands is $_{52}C_5 = \frac{52!}{5! \times 47!} = 2,598,960$.

Sometimes it may be easier to calculate the possibility of something not happening, or the **complement of an event**. Represented by the symbol $\bar{A}$, the complement of A is the probability that event A does not happen. When you know the probability of event A occurring, you can use the formula $P(\bar{A}) = 1 - P(A)$, where $P(\bar{A})$ is the probability of event A not occurring, and $P(A)$ is the probability of event A occurring.

The **addition rule** for probability is used for finding the probability of a compound event. Use the formula $P(A \text{ or } B) = P(A) + P(B) - P(A \text{ and } B)$, where $P(A)$ is the probability of the event A occurring, $P(B)$ is the probability of event B occurring, and $P(A \text{ and } B)$ is the probability of both events occurring to find the probability of a compound event. The probability of both events occurring at the same time must be subtracted to eliminate any overlap in the first two probabilities.

Conditional probability is the probability of a dependent event occurring once the original event has already occurred. Given event A and dependent event B, the probability of event B occurring when event A has already occurred is represented by the notation $P(A|B)$. To find the probability of event B occurring, take into account the fact that event A has already occurred and adjust the total number of possible outcomes. For example, suppose you have ten balls numbered 1–10 and you want ball number 7 to be pulled in two pulls. On the first pull, the probability of getting the 7 is $\frac{1}{10}$ because there is one ball with a 7 on it and 10 balls to choose from. Assuming the first pull did not yield a 7, the probability of pulling a 7 on the second pull is now $\frac{1}{9}$ because there are only 9 balls remaining for the second pull.

The **multiplication rule** can be used to find the probability of two independent events occurring using the formula $P(A \text{ and } B) = P(A) \, P(B)$, where $P(A \text{ and } B)$ is the probability of two independent events occurring, $P(A)$ is the probability of the first event occurring, and $P(B)$ is the probability of the second event occurring.

The multiplication rule can also be used to find the probability of two dependent events occurring using the formula $P(A \text{ and } B) = P(A) \cdot P(B|A)$, where $P(A \text{ and } B)$ is the probability of two dependent events occurring, $P(A)$ is the probability of the first event occurring, and $P(B|A)$ is the probability of the second event occurring after the first event has already occurred.

Before using the multiplication rule, you MUST first determine whether the two events are dependent or independent.

Use a combination of the multiplication rule and the rule of complements to find the probability that at least one outcome of the element will occur. This given by the general formula $P(\text{at least one event occurring}) = 1 - P(\text{no outcomes occurring})$. For example, to find the probability that at least one even number will show when a pair of dice is rolled, find the probability that two odd numbers will be rolled (no even numbers) and subtract from one. You can always use a tree diagram or make a chart to list the possible outcomes when the sample space is small, such as in the dice-rolling example, but in most cases it will be much faster to use the multiplication and complement formulas.

Expected value is a method of determining expected outcome in a random situation. It is really a sum of the weighted probabilities of the possible outcomes. Multiply the probability of an event occurring by the weight assigned to that probability (such as the amount of money won or lost). A practical application of the expected value is to determine whether a game of chance is really fair. If the sum of the weighted probabilities is equal to zero, the game is generally considered fair because the player has a fair chance to at least to break even. If the expected value is less than zero, then players lose more than they win. For example, a lottery drawing might allow the player to choose any three-digit number, 000–999. The probability of choosing the winning number is 1:1000. If it costs $1 to play, and a winning number receives $500, the expected value is $\left(-\$1 \cdot \frac{999}{1,000}\right) + \left(\$500 \cdot \frac{1}{1,000}\right) = -0.499$ or $-\$0.50$. You can expect to lose on average 50 cents for every dollar you spend.

Most of the time, when we talk about probability, we mean theoretical probability. **Experimental probability**, or empirical probability or relative frequency, is the number of times an outcome occurs in a particular experiment or a certain number of observed events. While theoretical probability is based on what *should* happen, experimental probability is based on what *has* happened. Experimental probability is calculated in the same way as theoretical, except that actual outcomes are used instead of possible outcomes.

Theoretical and experimental probability do not always line up with one another. Theoretical probability says that out of 20 coin tosses, 10 should be heads. However, if we were actually to toss 20 coins, we might record just 5 heads. This doesn't mean that our theoretical probability is incorrect; it just means that this particular experiment had results that were different from what was predicted. A practical application of empirical probability is the insurance industry. There are no set functions that define life span, health, or safety. Insurance companies look at factors from hundreds of thousands of individuals to find patterns that they then use to set the formulas for insurance premiums.

Objective probability is based on mathematical formulas and documented evidence. Examples of objective probability include raffles or lottery drawings where there is a pre-determined number of possible outcomes and a predetermined number of outcomes that correspond to an event. Other cases of objective probability include probabilities of rolling dice, flipping coins, or drawing cards. Most gambling games are based on objective probability.

Subjective probability is based on personal or professional feelings and judgments. Often, there is a lot of guesswork following extensive research. Areas where subjective probability is applicable include sales trends and business expenses. Attractions set admission prices based on subjective probabilities of attendance based on varying admission rates in an effort to maximize their profit.

Common Charts and Graphs

A bar graph is a graph that uses bars to compare data, as if each bar were a ruler being used to measure the data. The graph includes a scale that identifies the units being measured.

A line graph is a graph that connects points to show how data increases or decreases over time. The time line is the horizontal axis. The connecting lines between data points on the graph are a way to more clearly show how the data changes.

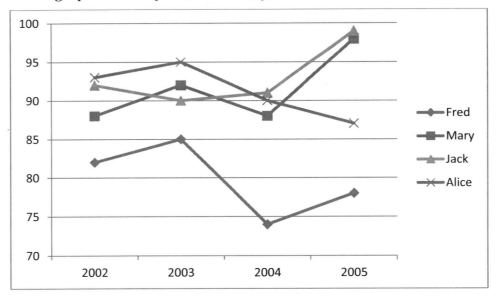

A pictograph is a graph that uses pictures or symbols to show data. The pictograph will have a key to identify what each symbol represents. Generally, each symbol stands for one or more objects.

A pie chart or circle graph is a diagram used to compare parts of a whole. The full pie represents the whole, and it is divided into sectors that each represent something that is a part of the whole. Each sector or slice of the pie is either labeled to indicate what it represents, or explained on a key associated with the chart. The size of each slice is determined by the percentage of the whole that the associated quantity represents. Numerically, the angle measurement of each sector can be computed by solving the proportion: x/360 = part/whole.

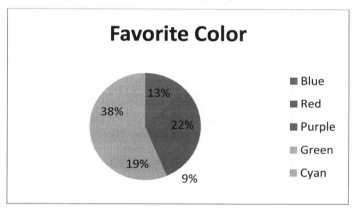

A histogram is a special type of bar graph where the data are grouped in intervals (for example 20-29, 30-39, 40-49, etc.). The frequency, or number of times a value occurs in each interval, is indicated by the height of the bar. The intervals do not have to be the same amount but usually are (all data in ranges of 10 or all in ranges of 5, for example). The smaller the intervals, the more detailed the information.

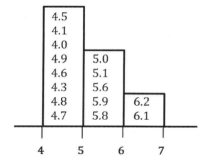

A stem-and-leaf plot is a way to organize data visually so that the information is easy to understand. A stem-and-leaf plot is simple to construct because a simple line separates the stem (the part of the plot listing the tens digit, if displaying two-digit data) from the leaf (the part that shows the ones digit). Thus, the number 45 would appear as 4 | 5. The stem-and-leaf plot for test scores of a group of 11 students might look like the following:

9 | 5
8 | 1, 3, 8
7 | 0, 2, 4, 6, 7
6 | 2, 8

A stem-and-leaf plot is similar to a histogram or other frequency plot, but with a stem-and-leaf plot, all the original data is preserved. In this example, it can be seen at a glance that nearly half the students scored in the 70's, yet all the data has been maintained. These plots can be used for larger numbers as well, but they tend to work better for small sets of data as they can become unwieldy with larger sets.

The Reading Test

The 30 minute EXPLORE Reading Test consists of reading selections, each followed by 10 questions. Some of the selections are drawn from the humanities, some from social studies, and some from prose fiction.

Understanding Literature

Reading literature is a different experience than reading non-fiction works. Our imagination is more active as we review what we have read, imagine ourselves as characters in the novel, and try to guess what will happen next. Suspense, surprise, fantasy, fear, anxiety, compassion, and a host of other emotions and feelings may be stirred by a provocative novel.

Reading longer works of fiction is a cumulative process. Some elements of a novel have a great impact, while others may go virtually unnoticed. Therefore, as novels are read with a critical eye to language, it is helpful to perceive and identify larger patterns and movements in the work as a whole. This will benefit the reader by placing characters and events in perspective, and will enrich the reading experience greatly. Novels should be savored rather than gulped. Careful reading and thoughtful analysis of the major themes of the novel are essential to a clear understanding of the work.

One of the most important skills in reading comprehension is the identification of **topics** and **main ideas.** There is a subtle difference between these two features. The topic is the subject of a text, or what the text is about. The main idea, on the other hand, is the most important point being made by the author. The topic is usually expressed in a few words at the most, while the main idea often needs a full sentence to be completely defined. As an example, a short passage might have the

- 48 -

topic of penguins and the main idea *Penguins are different from other birds in many ways.* In most nonfiction writing, the topic and the main idea will be stated directly, often in a sentence at the very beginning or end of the text. When being tested on an understanding of the author's topic, the reader can quickly *skim* the passage for the general idea, stopping to read only the first sentence of each paragraph. A paragraph's first sentence is often (but not always) the main topic sentence, and it gives you a summary of the content of the paragraph. However, there are cases in which the reader must figure out an unstated topic or main idea. In these instances, the student must read every sentence of the text, and try to come up with an overarching idea that is supported by each of those sentences.

While the main idea is the overall premise of a story, **supporting details** provide evidence and backing for the main point. In order to show that a main idea is correct, or valid, the author needs to add details that prove their point. All texts contain details, but they are only classified as supporting details when they serve to reinforce some larger point. Supporting details are most commonly found in informative and persuasive texts. In some cases, they will be clearly indicated with words like *for example* or *for instance*, or they will be enumerated with words like *first*, *second*, and *last*. However, they may not be indicated with special words. As a reader, it is important to consider whether the author's supporting details really back up his or her main point. Supporting details can be factual and correct but still not relevant to the author's point. Conversely, supporting details can seem pertinent but be ineffective because they are based on opinion or assertions that cannot be proven.

An example of a main idea is: "Giraffes live in the Serengeti of Africa." A supporting detail about giraffes could be: "A giraffe uses its long neck to reach twigs and leaves on trees." The main idea gives the general idea that the text is about giraffes. The supporting detail gives a specific fact about how the giraffes eat.

As opposed to a main idea, themes are seldom expressed directly in a text, so they can be difficult to identify. A **theme** is an issue, an idea, or a question raised by the text. For instance, a theme of William Shakespeare's *Hamlet* is indecision, as the title character explores his own psyche and the results of his failure to make bold choices. A great work of literature may have many themes, and the reader is justified in identifying any for which he or she can find support. One common characteristic of themes is that they raise more questions than they answer. In a good piece of fiction, the author is not always trying to convince the reader, but is instead trying to elevate the reader's perspective and encourage him to consider the themes more deeply. When reading, one can identify themes by constantly asking what general issues the text is addressing. A good way to evaluate an author's approach to a theme is to begin reading with a question in mind (for example, how does this text approach the theme of love?) and then look for evidence in the text that addresses that question.

Purposes for Writing

In order to be an effective reader, one must pay attention to the author's **position** and purpose. Even those texts that seem objective and impartial, like textbooks, have some sort of position and bias. Readers need to take these positions into account when considering the author's message. When an author uses emotional language or clearly favors one side of an argument, his position is clear. However, the author's position may be evident not only in what he writes, but in what he doesn't write. For this reason, it is sometimes necessary to review some other texts on the same topic in order to develop a view of the author's position. If this is not possible, then it may be useful to acquire a little background personal information about the author. When the only source of information is the text, however, the reader should look for language and argumentation that seems to indicate a particular stance on the subject.

Identifying the **purpose** of an author is usually easier than identifying her position. In most cases, the author has no interest in hiding his or her purpose. A text that is meant to entertain, for instance, should be obviously written to please the reader. Most narratives, or stories, are written to entertain, though they may also inform or persuade. Informative texts are easy to identify as well. The most difficult purpose of a text to identify is persuasion, because the author has an interest in making this purpose hard to detect. When a person knows that the author is trying to convince him, he is automatically more wary and skeptical of the argument. For this reason persuasive texts often try to establish an entertaining tone, hoping to amuse the reader into agreement, or an informative tone, hoping to create an appearance of authority and objectivity.

An author's purpose is often evident in the organization of the text. For instance, if the text has headings and subheadings, if key terms are in bold, and if the author makes his main idea clear from the beginning, then the likely purpose of the text is to inform. If the author begins by making a claim and then makes various arguments to support that claim, the purpose is probably to persuade. If the author is telling a story, or is more interested in holding the attention of the reader than in making a particular point or delivering information, then his purpose is most likely to entertain. As a reader, it is best to judge an author on how well he accomplishes his purpose. In other words, it is not entirely fair to complain that a textbook is boring: if the text is clear and easy to understand, then the author has done his job. Similarly, a storyteller should not be judged too harshly for getting some facts wrong, so long as he is able to give pleasure to the reader.

The author's purpose for writing will affect his writing style and the response of the reader. In a **persuasive essay**, the author is attempting to change the reader's mind or convince him of something he did not believe previously. There are several identifying characteristics of persuasive writing. One is opinion presented as fact. When an author attempts to persuade the reader, he often presents his or her opinions as if they were fact. A reader must be on guard for statements that sound factual but which cannot be subjected to research, observation, or experiment. Another characteristic of persuasive writing is emotional language. An author will often try to play on the reader's emotion by appealing to his sympathy or sense of morality. When an author uses colorful or evocative language with the intent of arousing the reader's passions, it is likely that he is attempting to persuade. Finally, in many cases a persuasive text will give an unfair explanation of opposing positions, if these positions are mentioned at all.

An **informative text** is written to educate and enlighten the reader. Informative texts are almost always nonfiction, and are rarely structured as a story. The intention of an informative text is to deliver information in the most comprehensible way possible, so the structure of the text is likely to be very clear. In an informative text, the thesis statement is often in the first sentence. The author may use some colorful language, but is likely to put more emphasis on clarity and precision. Informative essays do not typically appeal to the emotions. They often contain facts and figures, and rarely include the opinion of the author. Sometimes a persuasive essay can resemble an informative essay, especially if the author maintains an even tone and presents his or her views as if they were established fact.

The success or failure of an author's intent to **entertain** is determined by those who read the author's work. Entertaining texts may be either fiction or nonfiction, and they may describe real or imagined people, places, and events. Entertaining texts are often narratives, or stories. A text that is written to entertain is likely to contain colorful language that engages the imagination and the emotions. Such writing often features a great deal of figurative language, which typically enlivens its subject matter with images and analogies. Though an entertaining text is not usually written to persuade or inform, it may accomplish both of these tasks. An entertaining text may appeal to the reader's emotions and cause him or her to think differently about a particular subject. In any case, entertaining texts tend to showcase the personality of the author more so than do other types of writing.

When an author intends to **express feelings,** she may use colorful and evocative language. An author may write emotionally for any number of reasons. Sometimes, the author will do so because she is describing a personal situation of great pain or happiness. Sometimes an author is attempting to persuade the reader, and so will use emotion to stir up the passions. It can be easy to identify this kind of expression when the writer uses phrases like *I felt* and *I sense*. However, sometimes the author will simply describe feelings without introducing them. As a reader, it is important to recognize when an author is expressing emotion, and not to become overwhelmed by sympathy or passion. A reader should maintain some detachment so that he or she can still evaluate the strength of the author's argument or the quality of the writing.

In a sense, almost all writing is descriptive, insofar as it seeks to describe events, ideas, or people to the reader. Some texts, however, are primarily concerned with **description**. A descriptive text focuses on a particular subject, and attempts to depict it in a way that will be clear to the reader. Descriptive texts contain many adjectives and adverbs, words that give shades of meaning and create a more detailed mental picture for the reader. A descriptive text fails when it is unclear or vague to the reader. On the other hand, however, a descriptive text that compiles too much detail can be boring and overwhelming to the reader. A descriptive text will certainly be informative, and it may be persuasive and entertaining as well. Descriptive writing is a challenge for the author, but when it is done well, it can be fun to read.

Writing Devices

Authors will use different stylistic and writing devices to make their meaning more clearly understood. One of those devices is comparison and contrast. When an author describes the ways in which two things are alike, he or she is **comparing** them. When the author describes the ways in which two things are different, he or she is **contrasting** them. The "compare and contrast" essay is one of the most common forms in nonfiction. It is often signaled with certain words: a comparison may be indicated with such words as *both*, *same*, *like*, *too*, and *as well*; while a contrast may be indicated by words like *but*, *however*, *on the other hand*, *instead*, and *yet*. Of course, comparisons and contrasts may be implicit without using any such signaling language. A single sentence may both compare and contrast. Consider the sentence *Brian and Sheila love ice cream, but Brian prefers vanilla and Sheila prefers strawberry*. In one sentence, the author has described both a similarity (love of ice cream) and a difference (favorite flavor).

One of the most common text structures is **cause and effect**. A cause is an act or event that makes something happen, and an effect is the thing that happens as a result of that cause. A cause-and-effect relationship is not always explicit, but there are some words in English that signal causality, such as *since*, *because*, and *as a result*. As an example, consider the sentence *Because the sky was clear, Ron did not bring an umbrella*. The cause is the clear sky, and the effect is that Ron did not bring an umbrella. However, sometimes the cause-and-effect relationship will not be clearly noted. For instance, the sentence *He was late and missed the meeting* does not contain any signaling words, but it still contains a cause (he was late) and an effect (he missed the meeting). It is possible for a single cause to have multiple effects, or for a single effect to have multiple causes. Also, an effect can in turn be the cause of another effect, in what is known as a cause-and-effect chain.

Authors often use analogies to add meaning to the text. An **analogy** is a comparison of two things. The words in the analogy are connected by a certain, often undetermined relationship. Look at this analogy: moo is to cow as quack is to duck. This analogy compares the sound that a cow makes with the sound that a duck makes. Even if the word 'quack' was not given, one could figure out it is the correct word to complete the analogy based on the relationship between the words 'moo' and 'cow'. Some common relationships for analogies include synonyms, antonyms, part to whole, definition, and actor to action.

Another element that impacts a text is the author's point of view. The **point of view** of a text is the perspective from which it is told. The author will always have a point of view about a story before he draws up a plot line. The author will know what events they want to take place, how they want the characters to interact, and how the story will resolve. An author will also have an opinion on the topic, or series of events, which is presented in the story, based on their own prior experience and beliefs.

The two main points of view that authors use are first person and third person. If the narrator of the story is also the main character, or *protagonist*, the text is written in first-person point of view. In first person, the author writes with the word *I*. Third-person point of view is probably the most common point of view that authors use. Using third person, authors refer to each character using the words *he* or *she*. In third-person omniscient, the narrator is not a character in the story and tells the story of all of the characters at the same time.

A good writer will use **transitional words** and phrases to guide the reader through the text. You are no doubt familiar with the common transitions, though you may never have considered how they operate. Some transitional phrases (*after, before, during, in the middle of*) give information about time. Some indicate that an example is about to be given (*for example, in fact, for instance*). Writers use them to compare (*also, likewise*) and contrast (*however, but, yet*). Transitional words and phrases can suggest addition (*and, also, furthermore, moreover*) and logical relationships (*if, then, therefore, as a result, since*). Finally, transitional words and phrases can demarcate the steps in a process (*first, second, last*). You should incorporate transitional words and phrases where they will orient your reader and illuminate the structure of your composition.

Types of Passages

A **narrative** passage is a story. Narratives can be fiction or nonfiction. However, there are a few elements that a text must have in order to be classified as a narrative. To begin with, the text must have a plot. That is, it must describe a series of events. If it is a good narrative, these events will be interesting and emotionally engaging to the reader. A narrative also has characters. These could be people, animals, or even inanimate objects, so long as they participate in the plot. A narrative passage often contains figurative language, which is meant to stimulate the imagination of the reader by making comparisons and observations. A metaphor, which is a description of one thing in terms of another, is a common piece of figurative language. *The moon was a frosty snowball* is an example of a metaphor: it is obviously untrue in the literal sense, but it suggests a certain mood for the reader. Narratives often proceed in a clear sequence, but they do not need to do so.

An **expository** passage aims to inform and enlighten the reader. It is nonfiction and usually centers around a simple, easily defined topic. Since the goal of exposition is to teach, such a passage should be as clear as possible. It is common for an expository passage to contain helpful organizing words, like *first*, *next*, *for example*, and *therefore*. These words keep the reader oriented in the text. Although expository passages do not need to feature colorful language and artful writing, they are often more effective when they do. For a reader, the challenge of expository passages is to maintain steady attention. Expository passages are not always about subjects in which a reader will naturally be interested, and the writer is often more concerned with clarity and comprehensibility than with engaging the reader. For this reason, many expository passages are dull. Making notes is a good way to maintain focus when reading an expository passage.

A **technical** passage is written to describe a complex object or process. Technical writing is common in medical and technological fields, in which complicated mathematical, scientific, and engineering ideas need to be explained simply and clearly. To ease comprehension, a technical passage usually proceeds in a very logical order. Technical passages often have clear headings and subheadings, which are used to keep the reader oriented in the text. It is also common for these passages to break sections up with numbers or letters. Many technical passages look more like an outline than a piece of prose. The amount of jargon or difficult vocabulary will vary in a technical passage depending on the intended audience. As much as possible, technical passages try to avoid language that the reader will have to research in order to understand the message. Of course, it is not always possible to avoid jargon.

A **persuasive** passage is meant to change the reader's mind or lead her into agreement with the author. The persuasive intent may be obvious, or it may be quite difficult to discern. In some cases, a persuasive passage will be indistinguishable from an informative passage: it will make an assertion and offer supporting details. However, a persuasive passage is more likely to make claims based on opinion and to appeal to the reader's emotions. Persuasive passages may not describe alternate positions and, when they do, they often display significant bias. It may be clear that a persuasive passage is giving the author's viewpoint, or the passage may adopt a seemingly objective tone. A persuasive passage is successful if it can make a convincing argument and win the trust of the reader.

A persuasive essay will likely focus on one central argument, but it may make many smaller claims along the way. These are subordinate arguments with which the reader must agree if he or she is going to agree with the central argument. The central argument will only be as strong as the subordinate claims. These claims should be rooted in fact and observation, rather than subjective judgment. The best persuasive essays provide enough supporting detail to justify claims without overwhelming the reader. Remember that a fact must be susceptible to independent verification: that is, it must be something the reader could confirm. Also, statistics are only effective when they take into account possible objections. For instance, a statistic on the number of foreclosed houses would only be useful if it was taken over a defined interval and in a defined area. Most readers are wary of statistics, because they are so often misleading. If possible, a persuasive essay should always include references so that the reader can obtain more information. Of course, this means that the writer's accuracy and fairness may be judged by the inquiring reader.

Opinions are formed by emotion as well as reason, and persuasive writers often appeal to the feelings of the reader. Although readers should always be skeptical of this technique, it is often used in a proper and ethical manner. For instance, there are many subjects that have an obvious emotional component, and therefore cannot be completely treated without an appeal to the emotions. Consider an article on drunk driving: it makes sense to include some specific examples that will alarm or sadden the reader. After all, drunk driving often has serious and tragic consequences. Emotional appeals are not appropriate, however, when they attempt to mislead the reader. For instance, in political advertisements it is common to emphasize the patriotism of the preferred candidate, because this will encourage the audience to link their own positive feelings about the country with their opinion of the candidate. However, these ads often imply that the other candidate is unpatriotic, which in most cases is far from the truth. Another common and improper emotional appeal is the use of loaded language, as for instance referring to an avidly religious person as a "fanatic" or a passionate environmentalist as a "tree hugger." These terms introduce an emotional component that detracts from the argument.

History and Culture

Historical context has a profound influence on literature: the events, knowledge base, and assumptions of an author's time color every aspect of his or her work. Sometimes, authors hold opinions and use language that would be considered inappropriate or immoral in a modern setting, but that was acceptable in the author's time. As a reader, one should consider how the historical context influenced a work and also how today's opinions and ideas shape the way modern readers read the works of the past. For instance, in most societies of the past, women were treated as second-class citizens. An author who wrote in 18th-century England might sound sexist to modern readers, even if that author was relatively feminist in his time. Readers should not have to excuse the faulty assumptions and prejudices of the past, but they should appreciate that a person's thoughts and words are, in part, a result of the time and culture in which they live or lived, and it is perhaps unfair to expect writers to avoid all of the errors of their times.

Even a brief study of world literature suggests that writers from vastly different cultures address similar themes. For instance, works like the *Odyssey* and *Hamlet* both tackle the individual's battle for self-control and independence. In every culture, authors address themes of personal growth and the struggle for maturity. Another universal theme is the conflict between the individual and society. In works as culturally disparate as *Native Son*, the *Aeneid*, and *1984*, authors dramatize how people struggle to maintain their personalities and dignity in large, sometimes oppressive groups. Finally, many cultures have versions of the hero's (or heroine's) journey, in which an adventurous person must overcome many obstacles in order to gain greater knowledge, power, and perspective. Some famous works that treat this theme are the *Epic of Gilgamesh*, Dante's *Divine Comedy*, and *Don Quixote.*

Authors from different genres (for instance poetry, drama, novel, short story) and cultures may address similar themes, but they often do so quite differently. For instance, poets are likely to address subject matter obliquely, through the use of images and allusions. In a play, on the other hand, the author is more likely to dramatize themes by using characters to express opposing viewpoints. This disparity is known as a dialectical approach. In a novel, the author does not need to express themes directly; rather, they can be illustrated through events and actions. In some regional literatures, like those of Greece or England, authors use more irony: their works have characters that express views and make decisions that are clearly disapproved of by the author. In Latin America, there is a great tradition of using supernatural events to illustrate themes about real life. In China and Japan, authors frequently use well-established regional forms (haiku, for instance) to organize their treatment of universal themes.

Responding to Literature

When reading good literature, the reader is moved to engage actively in the text. One part of being an active reader involves making predictions. A **prediction** is a guess about what will happen next. Readers are constantly making predictions based on what they have read and what they already know. Consider the following sentence: *Staring at the computer screen in shock, Kim blindly reached over for the brimming glass of water on the shelf to her side.* The sentence suggests that Kim is agitated and that she is not looking at the glass she is going to pick up, so a reader might predict that she is going to knock the glass over. Of course, not every prediction will be accurate: perhaps Kim will pick the glass up cleanly. Nevertheless, the author has certainly created the expectation that the water might be spilled. Predictions are always subject to revision as the reader acquires more information.

Test-taking tip: To respond to questions requiring future predictions, the student's answers should be based on evidence of past or present behavior.

Readers are often required to understand text that claims and suggests ideas without stating them directly. An **inference** is a piece of information that is implied but not written outright by the author. For instance, consider the following sentence: *Mark made more money that week than he had in the previous year*. From this sentence, the reader can infer that Mark either has not made much money in the previous year or made a great deal of money that week. Often, a reader can use information he or she already knows to make inferences. Take as an example the sentence *When his coffee arrived, he looked around the table for the silver cup.* Many people know that cream is typically served in a silver cup, so using their own base of knowledge they can infer that the subject of this sentence takes his coffee with cream. Making inferences requires concentration, attention, and practice.

Test-taking tip: While being tested on his ability to make correct inferences, the student must look for contextual clues. An answer can be *true* but not *correct*. The contextual clues will help you find the answer that is the best answer out of the given choices. Understand the context in which a phrase is stated. When asked for the implied meaning of a statement made in the passage, the student should immediately locate the statement and read the context in which it was made. Also, look for an answer choice that has a similar phrase to the statement in question.

A reader must be able to identify a text's **sequence**, or the order in which things happen. Often, and especially when the sequence is very important to the author, it is indicated with signal words like *first*, *then*, *next*, and *last*. However, sometimes a sequence is merely implied and must be noted by the reader. Consider the sentence *He walked in the front door and switched on the hall lamp*. Clearly, the man did not turn the lamp on before he walked in the door, so the implied sequence is that he first walked in the door and then turned on the lamp. Texts do not always proceed in an orderly sequence from first to last: sometimes, they begin at the end and then start over at the beginning. As a reader, it can be useful to make brief notes to clarify the sequence.

In addition to inferring and predicting things about the text, the reader must often **draw conclusions** about the information he has read. When asked for a *conclusion* that may be drawn, look for critical "hedge" phrases, such as *likely*, *may*, *can*, *will often*, among many others. When you are being tested on this knowledge, remember that question writers insert these hedge phrases to cover every possibility. Often an answer will be wrong simply because it leaves no room for exception. Extreme positive or negative answers (such as always, never, etc.) are usually not correct. The reader should not use any outside knowledge that is not gathered from the reading passage to answer the related questions. Correct answers can be derived straight from the reading passage.

Opinions, Facts, & Fallacies

Critical thinking skills are mastered through understanding various types of writing and the different purposes that authors have for writing the way they do. Every author writes for a purpose. Understanding that purpose, and how they accomplish their goal, will allow you to critique the writing and determine whether or not you agree with their conclusions.

Readers must always be conscious of the distinction between fact and opinion. A **fact** can be subjected to analysis and can be either proved or disproved. An **opinion**, on the other hand, is the author's personal feeling, which may not be alterable by research, evidence, or argument. If the author writes that the distance from New York to Boston is about two hundred miles, he is stating a fact. But if he writes that New York is too crowded, then he is giving an opinion, because there is no objective standard for overpopulation. An opinion may be indicated by words like *believe*, *think*, or *feel*. Also, an opinion may be supported by facts: for instance, the author might give the population density of New York as a reason for why it is overcrowded. An opinion supported by fact tends to be more convincing. When authors support their opinions with other opinions, the reader is unlikely to be moved.

Facts should be presented to the reader from reliable sources. An opinion is what the author thinks about a given topic. An opinion is not common knowledge or proven by expert sources, but it is information that the author believes and wants the reader to consider. To distinguish between fact and opinion, a reader needs to look at the type of source that is presenting information, what information backs-up a claim, and whether or not the author may be motivated to have a certain point of view on a given topic. For example, if a panel of scientists has conducted multiple studies on the effectiveness of taking a certain vitamin, the results are more likely to be factual than if a company selling a vitamin claims that taking the vitamin can produce positive effects. The company is motivated to sell its product, while the scientists are using the scientific method to prove a theory. If the author uses words such as "I think…", the statement is an opinion.

In their attempt to persuade, writers often make mistakes in their thinking patterns and writing choices. It's important to understand these so you can make an informed decision. Every author has a point of view, but when an author ignores reasonable counterarguments or distorts opposing viewpoints, she is demonstrating a **bias**. A bias is evident whenever the author is unfair or inaccurate in his or her presentation. Bias may be intentional or unintentional, but it should always alert the reader to be skeptical of the argument being made. It should be noted that a biased author may still be correct. However, the author will be correct in spite of her bias, not because of it. A **stereotype** is like a bias, except that it is specifically applied to a group or place. Stereotyping is considered to be particularly abhorrent because it promotes negative generalizations about people. Many people are familiar with some of the hateful stereotypes of certain ethnic, religious, and cultural groups. Readers should be very wary of authors who stereotype. These faulty assumptions typically reveal the author's ignorance and lack of curiosity.

Sometimes, authors will **appeal to the reader's emotion** in an attempt to persuade or to distract the reader from the weakness of the argument. For instance, the author may try to inspire the pity of the reader by delivering a heart-rending story. An author also might use the bandwagon approach, in which he suggests that his opinion is correct because it is held by the majority. Some authors resort to name-calling, in which insults and harsh words are delivered to the opponent in an attempt to distract. In advertising, a common appeal is the testimonial, in which a famous person endorses a product. Of course, the fact that a celebrity likes something should not really mean anything to the reader. These and other emotional appeals are usually evidence of poor reasoning and a weak argument.

Certain *logical fallacies* are frequent in writing. A logical fallacy is a failure of reasoning. As a reader, it is important to recognize logical fallacies, because they diminish the value of the author's message. The four most common logical fallacies in writing are the false analogy, circular reasoning, false dichotomy, and overgeneralization. In a **false analogy**, the author suggests that two things are similar, when in fact they are different. This fallacy is often committed when the author is attempting to convince the reader that something unknown is like something relatively familiar. The author takes advantage of the reader's ignorance to make this false comparison. One example might be the following statement: *Failing to tip a waitress is like stealing money out of somebody's wallet.* Of course, failing to tip is very rude, especially when the service has been good, but people are not arrested for failing to tip as they would for stealing money from a wallet. To compare stingy diners with thieves is a false analogy.

Circular reasoning is one of the more difficult logical fallacies to identify, because it is typically hidden behind dense language and complicated sentences. Reasoning is described as circular when it offers no support for assertions other than restating them in different words. Put another way, a circular argument refers to itself as evidence of truth. A simple example of circular argument is when a person uses a word to define itself, such as saying *Niceness is the state of being nice.* If the reader does not know what *nice* means, then this definition will not be very useful. In a text, circular reasoning is usually more complex. For instance, an author might say *Poverty is a problem for society because it creates trouble for people throughout the community.* It is redundant to say that poverty is a problem because it creates trouble. When an author engages in circular reasoning, it is often because he or she has not fully thought out the argument, or cannot come up with any legitimate justifications.

One of the most common logical fallacies is the **false dichotomy**, in which the author creates an artificial sense that there are only two possible alternatives in a situation. This fallacy is common when the author has an agenda and wants to give the impression that his view is the only sensible one. A false dichotomy has the effect of limiting the reader's options and imagination. An example of a false dichotomy is the statement *You need to go to the party with me, otherwise you'll just be bored at home.* The speaker suggests that the only other possibility besides being at the party is being bored at home. But this is not true, as it is perfectly possible to be entertained at home, or even to go somewhere other than the party. Readers should always be wary of the false dichotomy: when an author limits alternatives, it is always wise to ask whether he is being valid.

Overgeneralization is a logical fallacy in which the author makes a claim that is so broad it cannot be proved or disproved. In most cases, overgeneralization occurs when the author wants to create an illusion of authority, or when he is using sensational language to sway the opinion of the reader. For instance, in the sentence *Everybody knows that she is a terrible teacher*, the author makes an assumption that cannot really be believed. This kind of statement is made when the author wants to create the illusion of consensus when none actually exists: it may be that most people have a negative view of the teacher, but to say that *everybody* feels that way is an exaggeration. When a reader spots overgeneralization, she should become skeptical about the argument that is being made, because an author will often try to hide a weak or unsupported assertion behind authoritative language.

Two other types of logical fallacies are **slippery slope** arguments and **hasty generalizations**. In a slippery slope argument, the author says that if something happens, it automatically means that something else will happen as a result, even though this may not be true. (i.e., just because you study hard does not mean you are going to ace the test). "Hasty generalization" is drawing a conclusion too early, without finishing analyzing the details of the argument. Writers of persuasive texts often use these techniques because they are very effective. In order to **identify logical fallacies**, readers need to read carefully and ask questions as they read. Thinking critically means not taking everything at face value. Readers need to critically evaluate an author's argument to make sure that the logic used is sound.

Organization of the Text

The way a text is organized can help the reader to understand more clearly the author's intent and his conclusions. There are various ways to organize a text, and each one has its own purposes and uses.

Some nonfiction texts are organized to **present a problem** followed by a solution. In this type of text, it is common for the problem to be explained before the solution is offered. In some cases, as when the problem is well known, the solution may be briefly introduced at the beginning. The entire passage may focus on the solution, and the problem will be referenced only occasionally. Some texts will outline multiple solutions to a problem, leaving the reader to choose among them. If the author has an interest or an allegiance to one solution, he may fail to mention or may describe inaccurately some of the other solutions. Readers should be careful of the author's agenda when reading a problem-solution text. Only by understanding the author's point of view and interests can one develop a proper judgment of the proposed solution.

Authors need to organize information logically so the reader can follow it and locate information within the text. Two common organizational structures are cause and effect and chronological order. When using **chronological order**, the author presents information in the order that it happened. For example, biographies are written in chronological order; the subject's birth and childhood are presented first, followed by their adult life, and lastly by the events leading up to the person's death. In **cause and effect**, an author presents one thing that makes something else happen. For example, if one were to go to bed very late, they would be tired. The cause is going to bed late, with the effect of being tired the next day.

It can be tricky to identify the cause-and-effect relationships in a text, but there are a few ways to approach this task. To begin with, these relationships are often signaled with certain terms. When an author uses words like *because*, *since*, *in order*, and *so*, she is likely describing a cause-and-effect relationship. Consider the sentence, "He called her because he needed the homework." This is a simple causal relationship, in which the cause was his need for the homework and the effect was his phone call. Not all cause-and-effect relationships are marked in this way, however. Consider the sentences, "He called her. He needed the homework." When the cause-and-effect relationship is not indicated with a keyword, it can be discovered by asking why something happened. He called her: why? The answer is in the next sentence: He needed the homework.

Persuasive essays, in which an author tries to make a convincing argument and change the reader's mind, usually include cause-and-effect relationships. However, these relationships should not always be taken at face value. An author frequently will assume a cause or take an effect for granted. To read a persuasive essay effectively, one needs to judge the cause-and-effect relationships the author is presenting. For instance, imagine an author wrote the following: "The parking deck has been unprofitable because people would prefer to ride their bikes." The relationship is clear: the cause is that people prefer to ride their bikes, and the effect is that the parking deck has been unprofitable. However, a reader should consider whether this argument is conclusive. Perhaps there are other reasons for the failure of the parking deck: a down economy, excessive fees, etc. Too often, authors present causal relationships as if they are fact rather than opinion. Readers should be on the alert for these dubious claims.

Thinking critically about ideas and conclusions can seem like a daunting task. One way to make it easier is to understand the basic elements of ideas and writing techniques. Looking at the way different ideas relate to each other can be a good way for the reader to begin his analysis. For instance, sometimes writers will write about two different ideas that are in opposition to each other. The analysis of these opposing ideas is known as **contrast**. Contrast is often marred by the author's obvious partiality to one of the ideas. A discerning reader will be put off by an author who does not engage in a fair fight. In an analysis of opposing ideas, both

- 67 -

ideas should be presented in their clearest and most reasonable terms. If the author does prefer a side, he should avoid indicating this preference with pejorative language. An analysis of opposing ideas should proceed through the major differences point by point, with a full explanation of each side's view. For instance, in an analysis of capitalism and communism, it would be important to outline each side's view on labor, markets, prices, personal responsibility, etc. It would be less effective to describe the theory of communism and then explain how capitalism has thrived in the West. An analysis of opposing views should present each side in the same manner.

Many texts follow the **compare-and-contrast** model, in which the similarities and differences between two ideas or things are explored. Analysis of the similarities between ideas is called comparison. In order for a comparison to work, the author must place the ideas or things in an equivalent structure. That is, the author must present the ideas in the same way. Imagine an author wanted to show the similarities between cricket and baseball. The correct way to do so would be to summarize the equipment and rules for each game. It would be incorrect to summarize the equipment of cricket and then lay out the history of baseball, since this would make it impossible for the reader to see the similarities. It is perhaps too obvious to say that an analysis of similar ideas should emphasize the similarities. Of course, the author should take care to include any differences that must be mentioned. Often, these small differences will only reinforce the more general similarity.

Drawing Conclusions

Authors should have a clear purpose in mind while writing. Especially when reading informational texts, it is important to understand the logical conclusion of the author's ideas. **Identifying this logical conclusion** can help the reader understand whether he agrees with the writer or not. Identifying a logical conclusion is much like making an inference: it requires the reader to combine the information given by the text with what he already knows to make a supportable assertion. If a passage is written well, then the conclusion should be obvious even when it is unstated. If the author intends the reader to draw a certain conclusion, then all of his argumentation and detail should be leading toward it. One way to approach the task of drawing conclusions is to make brief notes of all the points made by the author. When these are arranged on paper, they may clarify the logical conclusion. Another way to approach conclusions is to consider whether the reasoning of the author raises any pertinent questions. Sometimes it will be possible to draw several conclusions from a passage, and on occasion these will be conclusions that were never imagined by the author. It is essential, however, that these conclusions be supported directly by the text.

The term **text evidence** refers to information that supports a main point or points in a story, and can help lead the reader to a conclusion. Information used as *text evidence* is precise, descriptive, and factual. A main point is often followed by supporting details that provide evidence to back-up a claim. For example, a story may include the claim that winter occurs during opposite months in the Northern and Southern hemispheres. *Text evidence* based on this claim may include countries where winter occurs in opposite months, along with reasons that winter occurs at different times of the year in separate hemispheres (due to the tilt of the Earth as it rotates around the sun).

Readers interpret text and respond to it in a number of ways. Using textual support helps defend your response or interpretation because it roots your thinking in the text. You are interpreting based on information in the text and not simply your own ideas. When crafting a response, look for important quotes and details from the text to help bolster your argument. If you are writing about a character's personality trait, for example, use details from the text to show that the character acted in such a way. You can also include statistics and facts from a nonfiction text to strengthen your response. For example, instead of writing, "A lot of people use cell phones," use statistics to provide the exact number. This strengthens your argument because it is more precise.

The text used to support an argument can be the argument's downfall if it is not credible. A text is **credible**, or believable, when the author is knowledgeable and objective, or unbiased. The author's motivations for writing the text play a critical role in determining the credibility of the text and must be evaluated when assessing that credibility. The author's motives should be for the dissemination of information. The purpose of the text should be to inform or describe, not to persuade. When an author writes a persuasive text, he has the motivation that the reader will do what they want. The extent of the author's knowledge of the topic and their motivation must be evaluated when assessing the credibility of a text. Reports written about the Ozone layer by an environmental scientist and a hairdresser will have a different level of credibility.

After determining your own opinion and evaluating the credibility of your supporting text, it is sometimes necessary to communicate your ideas and findings to others. When **writing a response to a text**, it is important to use elements of the text to support your assertion or defend your position. Using supporting evidence from the text strengthens the argument because the reader can see how in depth the writer read the original piece and based their response on the details and facts within that text. Elements of text that can be used in a response include: facts, details, statistics, and direct quotations from the text. When writing a response, one must make sure they indicate which information comes from the original text and then base their discussion, argument, or defense around this information.
A reader should always be drawing conclusions from the text. Sometimes conclusions are implied from written information, and other times the information is **stated directly** within the passage. It is always more comfortable to draw conclusions from information stated within a passage, rather than to draw them from mere implications. At times an author may provide some information and then describe a counterargument. The reader should be alert for direct statements that

are subsequently rejected or weakened by the author. The reader should always read the entire passage before drawing conclusions. Many readers are trained to expect the author's conclusions at either the beginning or the end of the passage, but many texts do not adhere to this format.

Drawing conclusions from information implied within a passage requires confidence on the part of the reader. **Implications** are things the author does not state directly, but which can be assumed based on what the author does say. For instance, consider the following simple passage: "I stepped outside and opened my umbrella. By the time I got to work, the cuffs of my pants were soaked." The author never states that it is raining, but this fact is clearly implied. Conclusions based on implication must be well supported by the text. In order to draw a solid conclusion, a reader should have multiple pieces of evidence, or, if he only has one, must be assured that there is no other possible explanation than his conclusion. A good reader will be able to draw many conclusions from information implied by the text, which enriches the reading experience considerably.

As an aid to drawing conclusions, the reader should be adept at **outlining** the information contained in the passage; an effective outline will reveal the structure of the passage, and will lead to solid conclusions. An effective outline will have a title that refers to the basic subject of the text, though it need not recapitulate the main idea. In most outlines, the main idea will be the first major section. It will have each major idea of the passage established as the head of a category. For instance, the most common outline format calls for the main ideas of the passage to be indicated with Roman numerals. In an effective outline of this kind, each of the main ideas will be represented by a Roman numeral and none of the Roman numerals will designate minor details or secondary ideas. Moreover, all supporting ideas and details should be placed in the appropriate place on the outline. An outline does not need to include every detail listed in the text, but it should feature all of those that are central to the argument or message. Each of these details should be listed under the appropriate main idea.

It is also helpful to **summarize** the information you have read in a paragraph or passage format. This process is similar to creating an effective outline. To begin with, a summary should accurately define the main idea of the passage, though it does not need to explain this main idea in exhaustive detail. It should continue by laying out the most important supporting details or arguments from the passage. All of the significant supporting details should be included, and none of the details included should be irrelevant or insignificant. Also, the summary should accurately report all of these details. Too often, the desire for brevity in a summary leads to the sacrifice of clarity or veracity. Summaries are often difficult to read, because they omit all of graceful language, digressions, and asides that distinguish great writing. However, if the summary is effective, it should contain much the same message as the original text.

Paraphrasing is another method the reader can use to aid in comprehension. When paraphrasing, one puts what they have read into their own words, rephrasing what the author has written to make it their own, to "translate" all of what the author says to their own words, including as many details as they can.

Test Taking Tips

Skimming

Your first task when you begin reading is to answer the question "What is the topic of the selection?" This can best be answered by quickly skimming the passage for the general idea, stopping to read only the first sentence of each paragraph. A paragraph's first is usually the main topic sentence, and it gives you a summary of the content of the paragraph.

Once you've skimmed the passage, stopping to read only the first sentences, you will have a general idea about what it is about, as well as what is the expected topic in each paragraph.

Each question will contain clues as to where to find the answer in the passage. Do not just randomly search through the passage for the correct answer to each question. Search scientifically. Find key word(s) or ideas in the question that are going to either contain or be near the correct answer. These are typically nouns, verbs, numbers, or phrases in the question that will probably be duplicated in the passage. Once you have identified those key word(s) or idea, skim the passage quickly to find where those key word(s) or idea appears. The correct answer choice will be nearby.

Example: What caused Martin to suddenly return to Paris?

The key word is Paris. Skim the passage quickly to find where this word appears. The answer will be close by that word.

However, sometimes key words in the question are not repeated in the passage. In those cases, search for the general idea of the question.

Example: Which of the following was the psychological impact of the author's childhood upon the remainder of his life?

Key words are "childhood" or "psychology". While searching for those words, be alert for other words or phrases that have similar meaning, such as "emotional effect" or "mentally" which could be used in the passage, rather than the exact word "psychology".

Numbers or years can be particularly good key words to skim for, as they stand out from the rest of the text.

Example: Which of the following best describes the influence of Monet's work in the 20th century?

20th contains numbers and will easily stand out from the rest of the text. Use 20th as the key word to skim for in the passage.

Other good key word(s) may be in quotation marks. These identify a word or phrase that is copied directly from the passage. In those cases, the word(s) in quotation marks are exactly duplicated in the passage.

Example: In her college years, what was meant by Margaret's "drive for excellence"?

"Drive for excellence" is a direct quote from the passage and should be easy to find.

Once you've quickly found the correct section of the passage to find the answer, focus upon the answer choices. Sometimes a choice will repeat word for word a portion of the passage near the answer. However, beware of such duplication – it may be a trap! More than likely, the correct choice will paraphrase or summarize the related portion of the passage, rather than being exactly the same wording.

For the answers that you think are correct, read them carefully and make sure that they answer the question. An answer can be factually correct, but it MUST answer the question asked. Additionally, two answers can both be seemingly correct, so be sure to read all of the answer choices, and make sure that you get the one that BEST answers the question.

Some questions will not have a key word.

Example: Which of the following would the author of this passage likely agree with?

In these cases, look for key words in the answer choices. Then skim the passage to find where the answer choice occurs. By skimming to find where to look, you can minimize the time required.

Sometimes it may be difficult to identify a good key word in the question to skim for in the passage. In those cases, look for a key word in one of the answer choices to skim for. Often the answer choices can all be found in the same paragraph, which can quickly narrow your search.

Paragraph Focus

Focus upon the first sentence of each paragraph, which is the most important. The main topic of the paragraph is usually there.

Once you've read the first sentence in the paragraph, you have a general idea about what each paragraph will be about. As you read the questions, try to determine which paragraph will have the answer. Paragraphs have a concise topic. The answer should either obviously be there or obviously not. It will save time if you can jump straight to the paragraph, so try to remember what you learned from the first sentences.

Example: The first paragraph is about poets; the second is about poetry. If a question asks about poetry, where will the answer be? The second paragraph.

The main idea of a passage is typically spread across all or most of its paragraphs. Whereas the main idea of a paragraph may be completely different than the main idea of the very next paragraph, a main idea for a passage affects all of the paragraphs in one form or another.

Example: What is the main idea of the passage?

For each answer choice, try to see how many paragraphs are related. It can help to count how many sentences are affected by each choice, but it is best to see how many paragraphs are affected by the choice. Typically the answer choices will include incorrect choices that are main ideas of individual paragraphs, but not the entire passage. That is why it is crucial to choose ideas that are supported by the most paragraphs possible.

Eliminate Choices

Some choices can quickly be eliminated. "Andy Warhol lived there." Is Andy Warhol even mentioned in the article? If not, quickly eliminate it.

When trying to answer a question such as "the passage indicates all of the following EXCEPT" quickly skim the paragraph searching for references to each choice. If the reference exists, scratch it off as a choice. Similar choices may be crossed off simultaneously if they are close enough.

In choices that ask you to choose "which answer choice does NOT describe?" or "all of the following answer choices are identifiable characteristics, EXCEPT which?" look for answers that are similarly worded. Since only one answer can be correct, if there are two answers that appear to mean the same thing, they must BOTH be incorrect, and can be eliminated.

Example Answer Choices:

A.)   changing values and attitudes

B.)   a large population of mobile or uprooted people

These answer choices are similar; they both describe a fluid culture. Because of their similarity, they can be linked together. Since the answer can have only one choice, they can also be eliminated together.

When presented with a question that offers two choices, or neither choice, or both choice, it is rarely both choices.

Example: When an atom emits a beta particle, the mass of the atom will:

A.   increase

B.   decrease.

C.   stay the same.

D.   either increase or decrease depending on conditions.

Answer D will rarely be correct, the answers are usually more concrete.

Contextual Clues

Look for contextual clues. An answer can be true but not correct. The contextual clues will help you find the answer that is most right and is correct. Understand the context in which a phrase is stated.

When asked for the implied meaning of a statement made in the passage, immediately go find the statement and read the context it was made in. Also, look for an answer choice that has a similar phrase to the statement in question.

Example: In the passage, what is implied by the phrase "Churches have become more or less part of the furniture"?

Find an answer choice that is similar or describes the phrase "part of the furniture" as that is the key phrase in the question. "Part of the furniture" is a saying that means something is fixed, immovable, or set in their ways. Those are all similar ways of saying "part of the furniture." As such, the correct answer choice will probably include a similar rewording of the expression.

Example: Why was John described as "morally desperate".

The answer will probably have some sort of definition of morals in it. "Morals" refers to a code of right and wrong behavior, so the correct answer choice will likely have words that mean something like that.

Fact/Opinion

When asked about which statement is a fact or opinion, remember that answer choices that are facts will typically have no ambiguous words. For example, how long is a long time? What defines an ordinary person? These ambiguous words of "long" and "ordinary" should not be in a factual statement. However, if all of the choices have ambiguous words, go to the context of the passage. Often a factual statement may be set out as a research finding.

Example: "The scientist found that the eye reacts quickly to change in light."

Opinions may be set out in the context of words like thought, believed, understood, or wished.

Example: "He thought the Yankees should win the World Series."

Time Management

In technical passages, do not get lost on the technical terms. Skip them and move on. You want a general understanding of what is going on, not a mastery of the passage.

When you encounter material in the selection that seems difficult to understand, bracket it. It often may not be necessary and can be skipped. Only spend time trying to understand it if it is going to be relevant for a question. Understand difficult phrases only as a last resort.

If low on time, save sequence questions that ask you to sequence four choices (I, II, III, IV) for last. They consume a lot of time. When you do work on them, first find the four sequences in the passages, and mark them I, II, III, and IV respectively. Look for transitional word cues in the sentences such as: first, initially, to start, early on, finally, in conclusion, in the end, or last. These transition words can help position the choices. Also, focus on eliminating the wrong choices. If you know that

- 78 -

a certain sequence must be first or last, then you can eliminate the choices that do not have that as an option.

Pace yourself. 9 minutes per passage, which is nearly a minute per question.

Do easy passages and questions first. The easier passages should be first.

Answer general questions before detail questions. A reader with a good understanding of the whole passage can often answer general questions without rereading a word. Get the easier questions out of the way before tackling the more time consuming ones.

Identify each question by type. Usually the wording of a question will tell you whether you can find the answer by referring directly to the passage or by using your reasoning powers. You alone know which question types you customarily handle with ease and which give you trouble and will require more time. Save the difficult questions for last.

Final Warnings

When asked for a conclusion that may be drawn, look for critical "hedge" phrases, such as likely, may, can, will often, sometimes, etc, often, almost, mostly, usually, generally, rarely, sometimes. Question writers insert these hedge phrases, to cover every possibility. Often an answer will be wrong simply because it leaves no room for exception.

Example: Animals live longer in cold places than animals in warm places.

This answer choice is wrong, because there are exceptions in which certain warm climate animals live longer. This answer choice leaves no possibility of exception. It states that every animal species in cold places live longer than animal species in warm places. Correct answer choices will typically have a key hedge word to leave room for exceptions.

Example: In severe cold, a polar bear cub is likely to survive longer than an adult polar bear.

This answer choice is correct, because not only does the passage imply that younger animals survive better in the cold, it also allows for exceptions to exist. The use of the word "likely" leaves room for cases in which a polar bear cub might not survive longer than the adult polar bear.

When asked how a word is used in the passage, don't use your existing knowledge of the word. The question is being asked precisely because there is some strange or unusual usage of the word in the passage. Go to the passage and use contextual clues to determine the answer. Don't simply use the popular definition you already know.

Stay alert for "switchbacks". These are the words and phrases frequently used to alert you to shifts in thought. The most common switchback word is "but". Others include although, however, nevertheless, on the other hand, even though, while, in spite of, despite, regardless of.

Once you know which paragraph the answer will be in, focus on that paragraph. However, don't get distracted by a choice that is factually true about the paragraph. Your search is for the answer that answers the question, which may be about a tiny aspect in the paragraph. Stay focused and don't fall for an answer that describes the larger picture of the paragraph. Always go back to the question and make sure you're choosing an answer that actually answers the question and is not just a true statement.

The Science Test

The Science test may scare you. For even the most accomplished student, most of the terms will be unfamiliar. General test-taking skill will help the most. DO NOT run out of time, move quickly, and use the easy pacing methods we outlined in the test-taking tactics section.

The most important thing you can do is to ignore your fears and jump into the test immediately- do not be overwhelmed by all of the strange-sounding terms. You have to jump into the test like jumping into a pool- all at once is the easiest way. Once you get past the jargon, you may find that the Science test is easier than even the Reading Test, but most students never finish the Science test. This is why managing your time on this test is at least as important as on the math test.

The test will have 6 sections. Each section is about the same difficulty. Some will be harder for you, of course, so plan ahead.

The test lasts 30 minutes; that's 5 minutes a section.

The first thing to do is to read the passage. Use 2 minutes to do this- really try to understand what's going on, treating all of the scientific terms as you would characters in a novel- just accept their names as they are, and follow the story. Use another 3 minutes to answer as many questions as you can; then, MOVE ON to the next section. It's important to answer all of the easy questions.

Overall, science is the test that is hardest to study for, and surprisingly, has the lowest test average for all test-takers, even lower than the Math. If science is a subject you take because you have to, and not because you want to, your primary goal on Science is damage control- keep it from dragging down your higher scores when EXPLORE averages your test scores to get the composite.

The Science test is also unlike any other science test you've probably ever taken in school. It's vital that you work a few practice SR tests before the test day- that alone will boost your score by 1-2 points if you've never taken the EXPLORE before.

Four Types of Passages

1. Graph Mania: 2 or more graphs with questions about their meaning. You should start by asking yourself basic questions including: What are the variables? What are the units of measure?, What are the values of the variables?, What are the trends?, and What are the correlations?.

2. Table Mania: 2 or more tables containing data, with questions about their meaning. You should start by asking yourself basic questions including: What are the variables? What are the units of measure?, What are the values of the variables?, What are the trends?, and What are the correlations?.

3. Fighting Scientists: 2 different theories are explained for a natural process, you answer questions about them. Short paragraphs will be provided representing the ideas of two scientists. They will disagree with each other. Your job is to analyze that argument and information in the two paragraphs. Approach it with the following questions. What is the nature of the disagreement? How has the opinion been reached? What forms of evidence might resolve the conflict? What are the points of agreement and disagreement? What evidence supports or denies support for either viewpoint?

4. Experiments: questions about data from experiments (usually 2) performed. Experiment descriptions will be provided, along with a statement of the experiment's results. You should start by asking yourself basic questions including: What is the experiment designed to find out?, What does the experimental method or any accompanying diagrams reveal? What are the variables? What are the controls? (Controls are precautions taken to eliminate all variables except the independent variable.) What are the results? Look for flaws in the experiment. Are the controls adequate? Is the conclusion justified by the data? Are the experimental errors so great as to invalidate the results? Once you thoroughly understand the

nature of the experiment and the meaning of the results, you should be able to deal with the multiple-choice questions based on the experiment.

Four Types of Questions

1. Fact: This question asks for a fact, usually some sort of number, based on the passage. For example, "what is the volume of the gas at 1 atmosphere?" followed by choices.

2. Graphs: This type asks you to pick between graphs that best represent something described in the question.

3. Short answer: This type requires a short answer, either a word or phrase that answers a question about the passage. This question is spotted not by the length of the answers (though they are usually short), but by how much "thought" is in the answer choice. For example, choices that read "Day 1 at 12:00 PM, Day 2 at 4:00 PM," etc., would be short answer even though they are long. The question is still looking for a simple fact.

4. Long answer: This question type is asking for an interpretation from the passage that requires you to decide between several possible extended answers.

There are three question difficulty levels: Understanding, analysis, and generalization. In each group of questions, the first ones will be understanding, then will come the analysis questions, and finally the generalization questions. These are in increasing levels of difficulty as the earlier questions ask easy-to-find answers, while the later questions involve greater depth of interpretation and the ability to draw conclusions from the data.

Answer Choice Elimination Techniques

Slang

Scientific sounding answers are better than slang ones. In the answer choices below, choice B is much less scientific and is incorrect, while choice A is a scientific analytical choice and is correct.

Example:

a.) To compare the outcomes of the two different kinds of treatment.

b.) Because some subjects insisted on getting one or the other of the treatments.

Extreme Statements

Avoid wild answers that throw out highly controversial ideas that are proclaimed as established fact. Choice A is a radical idea and is incorrect. Choice B is a calm rational statement. Notice that Choice B does not make a definitive, uncompromising stance, using a hedge word "if" to provide wiggle room.

Example:

a.) Bypass surgery should be discontinued completely.

b.) Medication should be used instead of surgery for patients who have not had a heart attack if they suffer from mild chest pain and mild coronary artery blockage.

Similar Answer Choices

When you have two answer choices that are direct opposites, one of them is usually the correct answer.

Example:

A.) The effectiveness of enzyme I at 30 degrees Celsius depends on its concentration.

B.) The effectiveness of enzyme II at 30 degrees Celsius depends on its concentration.

These two answer choices are very similar and fall into the same family of answer choices. A family of answer choices is when two or three answer choices are very similar. Often two will be opposites and one may show an equality.

Example:

A.) Operation I or Operation II can be conducted at equal cost

B.) Operation I would be less expensive than Operation II

C.) Operation II would be less expensive than Operation I

D.) Neither Operation I nor Operation II would be effective at preventing the spread of cancer.

Note how the first three choices are all related. They all ask about a cost comparison. Beware of immediately recognizing choices B and C as opposites and choosing one of those two. Choice A is in the same family of questions and should be considered as well. However, choice D is not in the same family of questions. It has nothing to do with cost and can be discounted in most cases.

Related to the family of answers concept are answer choices that have similar parts. Example:

A.) The first stage of reaction 1 and the first stage of reaction 2.

B.) The second stage of reaction 1 and the second stage of reaction 3.

C.) The second stage of reaction 1 and the second stage of reaction 2.

D.) The second stage of reaction 1 and the first stage of reaction 2.

In this question, answer choices B, C, and D all begin with the same phrase "the second stage of reaction 1". This means answer choice A can be eliminated. Then answer choices A and D both have the same phrase "the first stage of reaction 2". Also, answer choices B and C have different phrases. This means that either A or D is the correct answer. Since choice A has already been eliminated, D is probably the right answer. In these cases similar phrases identify answer choices as being members of the same family of answers. Each answer choice that has a similar phrase is in the same family of answers. Answer choices that fall into the most family of answers is usually the correct answer.

Once again, hedge words are usually good, while answer choices without hedge words are typically wrong. Answer choices that say "exactly", "always" are often wrong.

Time Management

Scan the passage to get a rough idea of what it is asking.

Avoid answers that, while obviously true, do not answer the question. Answers must ANSWER the question, not just be factually true statements. The answer choice must be based strictly on the contents of the passage and question.

Read all the choices. Later answer choices will often bring up a new point that you may not have considered. As you read the choices, scratch through the ones that you know are wrong, but don't make your final selection until you read them all.

The easier "understanding" questions are listed first. Do not skip these first questions in each group, though everywhere else (on other tests and in other questions in the science test that aren't the first question in a group) skip questions giving you too much difficulty. This is because if you don't understand the passage, you're in trouble on the latter questions. Make sure you know enough to get the first question right, because the other questions will all flow from a basic understanding of the passage.

Skip the hard questions that aren't the first question in a group.

If the answers are numerical, estimate. Calculation takes time, and you should avoid it whenever possible. You can usually eliminate three obviously wrong choices quite easily. For example, suppose a graph shows that an object has traveled 48 meters in 11 seconds, and you are asked to find its speed. You are given these choices:

a. 250 m/s

b. 42 m/s

c. 4.4 m/s

d. 1.2 m/s

You know that 48 divided by 11 will be a little over 4, so you can pick out C as the answer without ever doing the calculation.

Highly Technical Questions May Not Be

Sometimes a single piece of information may be given to you. For example, blood velocity is lowest in the capillaries (averaging 3cm/sec).

A question may ask the following:

A physician examining a newly discovered tribe of people deep in the Amazon jungles found that the relative total surface area of their capillaries was greater than that previously reported for any other people. If the physician were to predict the average velocity of blood through their capillaries, which of the following values would be the most reasonable.

A.) 2 cm/sec
B.) 3 cm/sec
C.) 4 cm/sec
D.) 5 cm/sec

You know that 3 cm/sec is the standard, which is choice B. Without understanding any of the subject matter or even reading the associated graph, it is possible to choose the correct answer, which is A. The reason is because there is only answer, which is less than 3 cm/sec, while there are two answers that are greater than 3 cm/sec. Since you are not looking for an exact answer, but only a reasonable answer, then you can conclude that if the correct answer was greater than 3 cm/sec, TWO answer choices would meet that criteria. However, if the correct answer is less than 3 cm/sec, only ONE answer choice meets that criteria, meaning it is likely the correct answer.

Experiment Passages

The best way to remember three different but similar experiments is to focus on the differences between the experiments. Between the first and second experiment, what was changed? Between the second and third experiment, what was done differently? That will keep the overall experiments properly aligned in your mind. What variables changed between the experiments?

Random Tips

- On fact questions that require choosing between numbers, don't guess the smallest or largest choice unless you're sure of the answer (remember- "sure" means you would bet $5 on it).

- Short answer questions want you to choose between several words that are choices. Your best weapon on these is process of elimination- there are no easy tips.

- The long answer questions will often have a few "bizarre" choices, mentioning things that are not relevant to the passage. Also avoid answers that sound "smart." Again, if you're willing to bet $5, disregard the tips and go with your bet.

- In passages that describe a series of experiments, often the questions will ask you if the researcher made a mistake, or could improve the experiments by making some change; the answer choices will be two yes's and two no's, each with a different justification. Usually, the answer is one of the "no" choices- EXPLORE does not include deliberately flawed experiments in passages, so it is safe to assume that whatever suggestion the question poses would NOT improve the experiment. Of course, if you KNOW ($5 confidence) otherwise, disregard the tip.

- This bears repeating, especially on this test: you have probably never had a science test quite like the EXPLORE Science Test. More than any other test, you MUST take at least one practice test so as to not be bogged down with the unfamiliar format.

Appendix A: Area, Volume, Surface Area Formulas

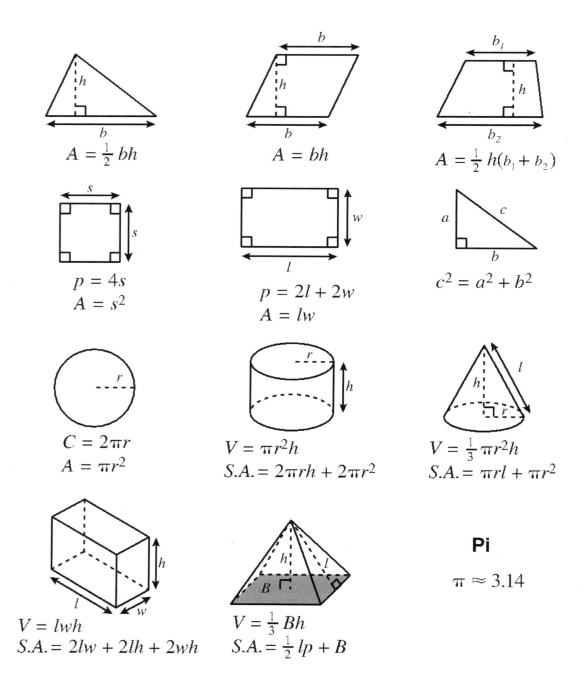

$A = \frac{1}{2}bh$

$A = bh$

$A = \frac{1}{2}h(b_1 + b_2)$

$p = 4s$
$A = s^2$

$p = 2l + 2w$
$A = lw$

$c^2 = a^2 + b^2$

$C = 2\pi r$
$A = \pi r^2$

$V = \pi r^2 h$
$S.A. = 2\pi rh + 2\pi r^2$

$V = \frac{1}{3}\pi r^2 h$
$S.A. = \pi rl + \pi r^2$

$V = lwh$
$S.A. = 2lw + 2lh + 2wh$

$V = \frac{1}{3}Bh$
$S.A. = \frac{1}{2}lp + B$

Pi

$\pi \approx 3.14$

English Test

Passage I

In 2001, 34% of the population of the United States was overweight. Problems of excessive weight (1)<u>would seem to be</u> associated with the wealth and (2)<u>more than sufficient</u> food supply. (3)<u>Much attention in recent years has been paid</u> to physical fitness and (4)<u>changing their diets</u> to become healthier. It seems logical that, with so much emphasis on health and nutrition, (5)<u>that</u> the solution to our nation's obesity problem would be in (6)<u>sight</u>. However, in a study of a population with moderate food insecurity, it was found that (7)<u>52%</u> were overweight. *Food insecurity* exists when the availability of nutritionally adequate and safe foods or the ability to acquire acceptable foods in socially acceptable ways is limited or uncertain. Over half of (8)the <u>United State's</u> population with a threat of hunger is overweight. Why would obesity be more prevalent among this group of people who have *fewer* resources?

Dieting and surgery do not address the problems of the economic groups with the most severe weight and nutrition problems. Surgery is expensive, and people with limited resources are (9)<u>still</u> not likely to buy expensive health foods when there are cheaper alternatives that satisfy (10)<u>your</u> hunger. The dollar menu at a fast food restaurant is certainly less expensive than preparing a well-balanced meal, (11)<u>and easier too</u>. Another reason for obesity in lower income groups is given by (12)<u>a theory called</u> the paycheck cycle theory. Most paychecks are distributed on a monthly basis, so if a family gets a paycheck, (13)<u>the family</u> will use these resources until they run out. Often money can be depleted before the next distribution. When this happens, there is an involuntary restriction of food. The hypothesis suggests (14)<u>that a</u> cycle of food restriction at the end of the month followed by bingeing that would promote weight gain. The main reasons for obesity and overweight in low-income groups (15)<u>would be</u> periodic food restriction and a poor diet because of financial restrictions.

Questions: Passage I

1.
    A.   NO CHANGE
    B.   are
    C.   seem to be
    D.   are not

2.
    F.   NO CHANGE
    G.   more, then sufficient
    H.   more, than sufficient
    J.   more-than-sufficient

3.
    A.   NO CHANGE
    B.   In recent years, much attention has been paid
    C.   Much attention, in recent years, has been paid
    D.   In recent years much attention

4.
    F.   NO CHANGE
    G.   diet
    H.   changing diet there
    J.   changing your diet

5.
    A.   NO CHANGE
    B.   OMIT the word
    C.   for
    D.   when

6.
    F.   NO CHANGE
    G.   site
    H.   cyte
    J.   cite

7.
    A.   NO CHANGE
    B.   52% of them
    C.   52% of the population
    D.   52% of it

8.
    F.   NO CHANGE
    G.   United States's
    H.   United States
    J.   United State

9.
    A.   NO CHANGE
    B.   OMIT word
    C.   often
    D.   frequently

10.
      F.   NO CHANGE
      G.   OMIT word
      H.   ones
      J.   the

11.
      A.   NO CHANGE
      B.   and easier to
      C.   and easier two
      D.   and easier, too

12.
      F.   NO CHANGE
      G.   OMIT expression
      H.   something called
      J.   a hypothesis called

13.
      A.   NO CHANGE
      B.   OMIT expression
      C.   they
      D.   someone

14.
      F   NO CHANGE
      G.   that
      H.   that there is
      J.   doing a

15.
      A.   NO CHANGE
      B.   are
      C.   seem to be
      D.   come from

Passage II

Volta Hall is a (1)<u>womens</u> residence located at the western side of campus. It
is composed of a (2)<u>porters</u> lodge, a small chapel, a dining hall, a library, a small laundry
service, a hair salon, a small (3)<u>convenient</u> store, and three residential buildings designated
for students.

Volta Hall has a total of three entry points that (4)<u>accesses</u> the entire structure. Two
of these entries are located on the sides of the dining hall and are left unlocked and
unprotected throughout the day. In the evening, usually (5)<u>some time</u> shortly after seven
o'clock, these (6)<u>entryways</u> are locked by Volta Hall personnel. This leaves only the main
entry, which is located at the front of the hall, (7)<u>as the only way</u> for individuals entering
and exiting the hall. No record is kept of students or other persons entering and exiting the
building. No identification is required to receive room keys from the porters. Security is so
lax that students (8)<u>have been known to even receive</u> more than one room key from the
porters and (9)<u>even</u> grab keys from behind the desk without giving notice.

The main entrance is guarded by two porters 24 hours (10)<u>out of each day</u>. The porters are
most alert during the morning and early afternoon. During the evening
(11)<u>hours</u> and early morning, the porters can be found sleeping. The main entry is usually
closed during the late evening and reopened in the morning. Although these doors are
closed, individuals have been known to open the latches from the outside, without forcing
them, to gain entry.

There are usually additional security guards on the second level. During the day, two
security guards are (12)<u>on watch or lack there of</u>. These guards are elderly men who have
been known to respond to incidents very slowly, have poor eyesight, are unarmed, (13)<u>and
physically out of shape</u>. Throughout the day and most of the evening, these guards can be
found asleep at their post. Only one guard is on duty during the evening hours. These men
can be found periodically walking around the perimeter of the building "checking" on
students.   These tactics have been (14)<u>proven to be</u> ineffective (15)<u>toward</u> criminal
incidents occurring within the hall.

Questions: Passage II

1.

    A.   NO CHANGE
    B.   woman's
    C.   women's
    D.   womens's

2.

    F.   NO CHANGE
    G.   porter
    H.   porter's
    J.   porters's

3.

    A.   NO CHANGE
    B.   OMIT word
    C.   convenience
    D.   connivance

4.

    F.   NO CHANGE
    G.   come into
    H.   come in to
    J.   provide access to

5.

    A.   NO CHANGE
    B.   OMIT expression
    C.   sometimes
    D.   a little

6.

    F.   NO CHANGE
    G.   entry ways
    H.   door ways
    J.   windows

7.

    A.   NO CHANGE
    B.   OMIT phrase
    C.   as the way
    D.   as the best way

8.

    F.   NO CHANGE
    G.   receive
    H.   have even been known to receive
    J.   get

9.

    A.   NO CHANGE
    B.   OMIT word
    C.   even to
    D.   to

10.

    F.   NO CHANGE
    G.   a day
    H.   at a time
    J.   on their shifts

11.

    A.   NO CHANGE
    B.   OMIT word
    C.   entrance
    D.   hour's

12.

    F.   NO CHANGE
    G.   on watch or lack thereof
    H.   supposedly on watch
    J.   not enough

13.

    A.   NO CHANGE
    B.   and out of shape
    C.   and are physically out of shape
    D.   and are out of shape

14.

    F.   NO CHANGE
    G.   OMIT expression
    H.   proved to be
    J.   tried to be

15.

    A.   NO CHANGE
    B.   OMIT word
    C.   when it comes to
    D.   in curbing

Passage III

Student Log Entry:

This is the first log entry for Mountain Maritime High (1)<u>School's</u> "Student Sailors" program. Our high school mascot is a sea lion, so we call ourselves the "Mountain Lions." We are going out on a university research vessel to collect water from the bottom of the Straits of San Juan.

Our journey began as we cruised over to Victoria on a ferry after a long flight. We were glad that the school paid for all of our transportation because we would have had to (2)<u>have done</u> a lot of car washes to (3)<u>have afforded</u> this trip. (4)<u>At last, we finally</u> boarded our ship on Vancouver Island and got settled in our berths. Soon we met the captain and crew, and (5)<u>soon</u> we were on our way. We sailed for several (6)<u>hours until</u> we arrived at the underwater Axial Volcano on the San Juan Ridge.

When we arrived, the Chief (7)<u>Scientist Dr. Ed Cook and his crew</u> got ready to collect the water samples. Soon, they were ready to cast out (8)<u>this</u> bundle of sampling bottles. The bottles close at any depth so that water can (9)<u>bring</u> back up to the lab. (10)<u>So far we have learned that</u> they are testing the water for trace metals such as iron, manganese, and helium isotopes.

The Axial Volcano erupted in 1998, and these tests (11)<u>will be used to detect</u> what the scientists call magmatic activity . We spoke with a scientist who is filtering the water to find (12)<u>these</u> tiny specks called teps. She thinks they ride up on the hot water plume that moves up from the vents. (13)<u>Last night</u> we were amazed at the marine life that comes up from the depths to see the lights on the (14)<u>ship and all</u>. There are so many marine scientists aboard that we had no trouble finding out (15)<u>what the names are</u> of what we saw.

Questions: Passage III

1.
- A. NO CHANGE
- B. schools
- C. Schools
- D. school's

2.
- F. NO CHANGE
- G. do
- H. did
- J. have

3.
- A. NO CHANGE
- B. have paid for
- C. afford
- D. have done

4.
- F. NO CHANGE
- G. At last, we
- H. Finally, at last we
- J. We at last

5.
- A. NO CHANGE
- B. sooner
- C. then
- D. lately

6.
- F. NO CHANGE
- G. hours, until
- H. hours and
- J. hours

7.
- A. NO CHANGE
- B. Scientist Dr. Ed Cook, and his crew
- C. Scientist, Dr. Ed Cook and his crew
- D. Scientist, Dr. Ed Cook, and his crew

8.
- F. NO CHANGE
- G. OMIT word
- H. a
- J. some

9.
- A. NO CHANGE
- B. brang
- C. be brought
- D. be brung

10.
    F.   NO CHANGE
    G.   OMIT phrase
    H.   So far, we have learned that
    J.   So far we have learned, that

Mathematics Test

1. Which of the following can be divided by 3, with no remainder?
    A. 2018
    B. 46
    C. 8912
    D. 555
    E. 739

2. A blouse normally sells for $138, but is on sale for 25% off. What is the cost of the blouse?
    F. $67
    G. $103.50
    H. $34.50
    J. $113
    K. $125

3. Which number equals 2^{-3}?
    A. ½
    B. ¼
    C. 1/8
    D. 1/16
    E. 1/12

4. A crane raises one end of a 3300 lb steel beam. The other end rests upon the ground. If the crane supports 30% of the beam's weight, how many pounds does it support?
    F. 330 lbs
    G. 990 lbs
    H. 700 lbs
    J. 1100 lbs
    K. 2310 lbs

5. What is the average of $\dfrac{7}{5}$ and 1.4 ?
    A. 5.4
    B. 1.4
    C. 2.4
    D. 7.4
    E. None of these

6. What is the surface area, in square inches, of a cube if the length of one side is 3 inches?
    F. 9
    G. 27
    H. 54
    J. 18
    K. 21

7. The following table shows the distance from a point to a moving car at various times.

d	Distance	50	70	110
t	Time	2	3	5

If the speed of the car is constant, which of the following equations describes the distance from the point to the car?

A. $d = 25\,t$
B. $d = 35\,t$
C. $d = 55\,t$
D. $d = 20\,t + 10$
E. None of these

8. A taxi service charges $5.50 for the first 1/5th of a mile, $1.50 for each additional 1/5th of a mile, and 20¢ per minute of waiting time. Joan took a cab from her place to a flower shop 8 miles away, where she bought a bouquet, then another 3.6 miles to her mother's place. The driver had to wait 9 minutes while she bought the bouquet. What was the fare?

F. $20
G. $120.20
H. $92.80
J. $91
K. $90

9. Which of the following expressions is equivalent to the equation $3x^2 + 4x - 15$?

A. $(x-3)(x+5)$
B. $(x+5)(3+x^2)$
C. $x(3x+4-15)$
D. $(3x^2+5)(x-5)$
E. $(x+3)(3x-5)$

10. Prizes are to be awarded to the best pupils in each class of an elementary school. The number of students in each grade is shown in the table, and the school principal wants the number of prizes awarded in each grade to be proportional to the number of students. If there are twenty prizes, how many should go to fifth grade students?

Grade	1	2	3	4	5
Students	35	38	38	33	36

F. 5
G. 4
H. 7
J. 3
K. 2

11. An MP3 player is set to play songs at random from the fifteen songs it contains in memory. Any song can be played at any time, even if it is repeated. There are 5 songs by Band A, 3 songs by Band B, 2 by Band C, and 5 by Band D. If the player has just played two songs in a row by Band D, what is the probability that the next song will also be by Band D?

    A. 1 in 5
    B. 1 in 3
    C. 1 in 9
    D. 1 in 27
    E. Not enough data to determine.

12. Referring again to the MP3 player described in Question 30, what is the probability that the next two songs will both be by Band B?

    F. 1 in 25
    G. 1 in 3
    H. 1 in 5
    J. 1 in 9
    K. Not enough data to determine.

13. Which of the following numbers is a prime number?

    A. 15
    B. 11
    C. 33
    D. 4
    E. 88

14. Evaluate the expression $(x - 2y)^2$ where x = 3 and y = 2.

    F. -1
    G. +1
    H. +4
    J. -2
    K. -3

15. Bob decides to go into business selling lemonade. He buys a wooden stand for $45 and sets it up outside his house. He figures that the cost of lemons, sugar, and paper cups for each glass of lemonade sold will be 10¢. Which of these expressions describes his cost for making g glasses of lemonade?

    A. $45 + $0.10*g
    B. $44.90*g
    C. $44.90*g+$0.10
    D. $90
    E. $45.10

16. To determine a student's grade, a teacher throws out the lowest grade obtained on 5 tests, averages the remaining grades, and round up to the nearest integer. If Betty scored 72, 75, 88, 86, and 90 on her tests, what grade will she receive?

    F. 68

    G. 85

    H. 88

    J. 84.8

    K. 84

17. There is a big sale on at the clothing store on Main Street. Everything is marked down by 33% from the original price, p. Which of the following expressions describes the sale price, S, to be paid for any item?

    A. $S = p - 0.33$

    B. $S = p - 0.33p$

    C. $S = 0.33p$

    D. $S = 0.33(1 - p)$

    E. $S = p + 0.33p$

18. A rock group with 5 musicians gets 25% of the gross sales of their new album, but they have to give their agent 15% of their share. If the album grosses $20,000,000, what is each band member's share?

    F. $850,000

    G. $4,000,000

    H. $1,150,000

    J. $650,000

    K. $800,000

19. Given the equation $\dfrac{3}{y-5} = \dfrac{15}{y+4}$, what is the value of y?

    A. 45

    B. 54

    C. $\dfrac{29}{4}$

    D. $\dfrac{4}{29}$

    E. $\dfrac{4}{45}$

20. The weight in pounds of five students is 112, 112, 116, 133, 145. What is the median weight of the group?

    F. 123.6

    G. 116

    H. 112

    J. 118.5

    K. 140

21. Which value is equivalent to 7.5×10^{-4}?
   A. 0.075
   B. 0.00075
   C. 0.0075
   D. 0.75
   E. 0.0030

22. How many real-number solutions exist for the equation $x^2 + 1 = 0$?
   F. 0
   G. 1
   H. 2
   J. 3
   K. 4

23. A bag contains six marbles: two green, two blue, and two red. If two marbles are drawn at random, what is the probability that they are of the same color?
   A. 3%
   B. 20%
   C. 25%
   D. 33%
   E. 5%

24. The number 5 is multiplied by its reciprocal. What is the result?
   F. 0
   G. 1
   H. 1/5
   J. 5
   K. -1

25. The sum of two negative numbers
   A. is always negative.
   B. is always positive.
   C. sometimes is positive and sometimes is negative/
   D. is always zero.
   E. none of the above

26. If an odd number is added to an even number, the result must be
   F. odd
   G. even
   H. positive
   J. zero
   K. prime

27. Richard sells cell phones. He is paid a commission of 10% for every phone he sells. The phones cost $140 each. How many phones must Richard sell in order to be paid $840?
    A. 40
    B. 50
    C. 60
    D. 70
    E. 84

28. A rectangular box is twice as long as it is wide. If it were 3 inches shorter and 3 inches wider, it would be square. What is the width in inches of the box?
    F. 4
    G. 6
    H. 8
    J. 12
    K. 24

29. If $3x + 5 = 11$, then $x = ?$
    A. 6
    B. 3
    C. 2
    D. 1
    E. 8

30. What is the fifth term in the arithmetic sequence 21, 17, 13, 9...
    F. 5
    G. 6
    H. 7
    J. 8
    K. 9

- 104 -

Reading Test

I. Prose Fiction:

This Passage Is A Re-Telling Of A Traditional American Indian Legend.
The Black Crow.

In ancient times, the people hunted the buffalo on the Great Plains. These huge animals were their source of food and clothing. With stone-tipped spears, they stalked the great beasts through the tall grasses. It was difficult and dangerous work, but they were forced to do it in order to survive.

At that time, there were many crows flying above the plains, as there are today. But unlike the crows we see now, these birds were white. And they were friends to the buffalo, which caused the hunters no end of travail. The white crows flew high above the plains, where they could see all that was happening below. And when they saw that hunters were approaching the herd, they would warn the buffalo. Swooping down low, they would land on the heads of the great beasts and call out to them: "Beware! Beware! Hunters are coming from the south! Caw, caw. Beware!" And the buffalo would stampede, leaving the hunters empty-handed.

This went on for some time, until the people were hungry, and something needed to be done. A council was convened, and the chief of the people spoke to them. "We must capture the chief of the crows, and teach him a lesson, he said. If we can frighten him, he will stop warning the buffalo when our hunters approach, and the other crows will stop as well."

The old chief then brought out a buffalo skin, one with the head and horns still attached. "With this, we can capture the chief of the crows," he said. And he gave the skin to one of the tribe's young braves, a man known as Long Arrow. "Disguise yourself with this, and hide among the buffalo in the herd," the chief told Long Arrow. "Then, when the chief of the crows approaches, you will capture him and bring him back to the tribe."

So Long Arrow donned the buffalo skin disguise and went out onto the plains. Carefully, he approached a large herd of buffalo and mingled among them, pretending to graze upon the grasses. He moved slowly with the herd as they sought fresh food, and he waited for the great white bird that was the chief of the crows.

The other braves made ready for the hunt. They prepared their stone-tipped spears and arrows, and they approached the grazing herd of beasts, hiding in ravines and behind rocks to try to sneak up on them. But the crows, flying high in the sky, saw everything. The chief of the crows saw the men in the ravines and tall grasses, and eventually he came gliding down to warn the buffalo of the approaching hunters.

Hearing the great white crow's warning, the herd ran from the hunters. All stampeded across the plains except Long Arrow, still in his disguise. Seeing that Long Arrow remained, and thinking that he was a buffalo like all the others, the great white crow flew to him and landed upon his head. "Caw, caw. Hunters are approaching! Have you not heard my warning? Why do you remain here?" But as the great bird cried out, Long Arrow reached from under his disguise and grabbed the bird's feet, capturing him. He pushed him into a rawhide bag and brought him back to the tribal council.

The people debated what to do with the chief of the crows. Some wanted to cut his wings, so that he could not fly. Some wanted to kill him, and some wanted to remove his feathers as punishment for making the tribe go hungry. Finally, one brave strode forward in anger, grabbed the rawhide bag that held the bird, and before anyone could prevent it, threw it into the fire.

As the fire burned the rawhide bag, the big bird struggled to escape. Finally, he succeeded in getting out of the bag and managed to fly out of the fire, but his feathers were singed and covered with black soot from the fire. The chief of the crows was no longer white; he was black – as crows are today.

And from that day forward, all crows have been black. And although they fly above the plains and can see all that transpires below, they no longer warn the buffalo that hunters are approaching.

QUESTIONS.

1. According to the passage, the people used stone spears to hunt the buffalo because
    A. They had no metal.
    B. They had no horses.
    C. They needed to eat.
    D. They were plentiful.

2. The word *travail* (Line 9) means
    F. Travel.
    G. Difficulty.
    H. Anger.
    J. Fear.

3. Which statement best describes what the chief of the crows represents in this passage?
    A. He symbolizes all that is evil.
    B. He is a symbol representing all crows.
    C. He represents the animal kingdom.
    D. He represents other predators who compete with the tribe.

4. Which of the following best describes the people's motivation for wanting to capture the chief of the crows?
    F. They hated birds.
    G. They wanted to turn him black.
    H. They wanted to eat him.
    J. They were hungry.

5. Long Arrow's activities among the herd while disguised imply that he
    A. Had time to kill.
    B. Wanted to fool the buffalo.
    C. Wanted to fool the crows.
    D. Had forgotten his stone-tipped spear.

6. In this tale, the rawhide bag and stone-tipped spears are both details that
    F. Are important for the outcome of the tale.
    G. Paint a picture of the primitive culture of the people.
    H. Make it clear that the people were dependent upon the buffalo.
    J. Show how the people hunted.

7. Why might the chief of the crows have landed upon Long Arrow's head after seeing the other buffalo stampede away?
    A. He thought his warning had not been heard.
    B. He wanted to see the disguise.
    C. He thought that Long Arrow was an injured buffalo.
    D. He had no fear of men.

8. Once the bird has been caught, what emotions are revealed by the people's deliberations about how to deal with him?
    F. Anger
    G. A calm resolve to change the birds' behavior
    H. A feeling of celebration now that the bird has been caught
    J. Hunger

9. What does the story tell us about why Long Arrow was selected for this task?
    A. He was the bravest man in the tribe.
    B. He was related to the chief.
    C. He was able to act like a buffalo.
    D. The story says nothing about why he was selected.

10. What does this story suggest that the American Indians thought of crows?
    F. They were dirty animals.
    G. They were clever animals.
    H. They were selfish animals.
    J. They disliked the people in the tribe.

II. Social Sciences:

This passage is adapted from "Sailing Around the World" by Capt. Joshua Slocum (1899).

I had not been in Buenos Aires for a number of years. The place where I had once landed from packets in a cart was now built up with magnificent docks. Vast fortunes had been spent in
remodeling the harbor; London bankers could tell you that. The port captain after assigning the *Spray* a safe berth with his compliments sent me word to call on him for anything I might want while in port and I felt quite sure that his friendship was sincere. The sloop was well cared for at Buenos Aires; her dockage and tonnage dues were all free, and the yachting fraternity of the city welcomed her with a good will. In town, I found things not so greatly changed as about the docks and I soon felt myself more at home.

From Montevideo I had forwarded a letter from Sir Edward Hairby to the owner of the "Standard", Mr Mulhall, and in reply to it was assured of a warm welcome to the warmest heart, I think, outside of Ireland. Mr Mulhall, with a prancing team, came down to the docks as soon as the Spray was berthed, and would have me go to his house at once, where a room was waiting. And it was New Year's day, 1896. The course of the *Spray* had been followed in the columns of the "Standard."

Mr Mulhall kindly drove me to see many improvements about the city, and we went in search of some of the old landmarks. The man who sold lemonade on the plaza when first I visited this wonderful city I found selling lemonade still at two cents a glass; he had made a fortune by it. His stock in trade was a wash tub and a neighboring hydrant, a moderate supply of brown sugar, and about six lemons that floated on the sweetened water. The water from time to time was renewed from the friendly pump. but the lemon "went on forever," and all at two cents a glass.

But we looked in vain for the man who once sold whisky and coffins in Buenos Aires; the march of civilization had crushed him -- memory only clung to his name. Enterprising man that he was, I fain would have looked him up. I remember the tiers of whisky barrels, ranged on end, on one side of the store, while on the other side, and divided by a thin partition, were the coffins in the same order, of all sizes and in great numbers. The unique arrangement seemed in order, for as a cask was emptied a coffin might be filled. Besides cheap whisky and many other liquors, he sold "cider" which he manufactured from damaged Malaga raisins. Within the scope of his enterprise was also the sale of mineral waters, not entirely blameless of the germs of disease. This man surely catered to all the tastes, wants, and conditions of his customers.

Farther along in the city, however, survived the good man who wrote on the side of his store, where thoughtful men might read and learn: "This wicked world will be destroyed by a comet! The owner of this store is therefore bound to sell out at any price and avoid the catastrophe." My friend Mr

Mulhall drove me round to view the fearful comet with streaming tail pictured large on the merchant's walls.

QUESTIONS.

1. The passage suggests that the *Spray* was
    A. A packet.
    B. A sailboat.
    C. A bus.
    D. A jet of water

2. The author found that, since his previous visit, the greatest changes in Buenos Aires had taken place:
    F. Downtown.
    G. At the harbor.
    H. At a lemonade stand.
    J. At the bank.

3. The author was shown around Buenos Aires by Mr. Mulhall. How did he come to know Mr. Mulhall?
    A. They had previously met in Ireland.
    B. They had met on the author's first visit to the city.
    C. They met through a letter of introduction.
    D. They met on the docks.

4. The passage suggests that the "Standard" was
    F. A steam packet.
    G. A sailboat.
    H. A newspaper.
    J. An ocean chart.

5. The author uses the term "landmarks" to refer to
    A. Monuments.
    B. Merchants.
    C. Banks.
    D. Buildings.

6. The passage suggests that the lemonade vendor used fresh lemons
    F. Whenever the flavor got weak.
    G. Every morning.
    H. Almost never.
    J. When he could get them.

7. The meaning of the word "fain" (Line 27) is closest to
    A. Anxiously.
    B. Willingly.
    C. Desperately.
    D. Indifferently.

8. The description of the mineral waters sold by the whiskey merchant (line 32) suggests that these waters

    F. Could cure disease.
    G. Were held in casks.
    H. Were not very clean.
    J. Were mixed with the cider.

9. The passage suggests that the merchant with the picture of the comet on his walls had

    A. Malaga raisins.
    B. Been in Buenos Aires when the author first visited.
    C. Painted the sign himself.
    D. Lived for a very long time.

10. The sign warning that a comet would cause the end of the world was most likely

    F. An advertising gimmick.
    G. A reflection of the merchant's paranoia.
    H. A way to cover an unsightly wall.
    J. Written about in the "Standard."

Ernst Lubitsch

The comedy of manners was a style of film popular in the 1930s. These movies expressed the frustrations of the depression-era poor by mocking the swells of the upper classes, and contrasting their gilded lives to the daily grind of the downtrodden masses. One of the greatest directors of this type of film was Ernst Lubitsch, a German filmmaker who eventually came to Hollywood to make some of his greatest films.

Lubitsch's film career began in the silent era. Born in Berlin, in 1982, he worked at first as an actor, subsequently debuting as a director with the film *Passion* in 1912. He made more than 40 films in Germany, but the advent of sound brought him to Hollywood, where the new technology was most readily available. After the producer Albert Zukor invited him to come to the U.S. in 1923, he pursued his career in the capital of film until the late 1940s. His signature style – a focus on seemingly insignificant details that imbued them with symbolism in the context of the film – was just as effective in the "talkies" as it had been in silent films. One of his greatest comedies, *Trouble in Paradise*, starred Herbert Marshall and Miriam Hopkins and was shot in 1932. A stinging social comedy that skewers the illusions of the upper classes, it would not have been well received in his native Germany of the time.

Trouble in Paradise tells the story of a charming, elegant thief. Marshall plays Gaston Monescu, a man whose charm and elegant manners allow him to work his way into the bosom of high society. In the hotels and clubs of the rich, he manages to gain the trust of wealthy individuals until he swindles them. Monescu courts the rich perfume heiress, Mariette, and we are never certain of how sincere his affection for her may be. But he is also in love with his accomplice, Lily, a clever thief in her own right. His eventual decision to leave Mariette for her can be seen as an affirmation of the unity of the working class in this very class-conscious film.

The opening scenes of the film provide a classic example of Lubitsch's wry symbolism. The opening shot is of a garbage can, which is duly picked up by a garbage man and dumped onto what seems to be a truck. But, as the camera pans back, we realize that the truck is, in fact, a gondola, and that the scene takes place in Venice. As the gondolier-garbage man breaks into a romantic song, the camera contrasts the elegant city, it's palaces and beautiful canals, with the mundane reality of garbage and necessary, low-wage work.

The film continues to contrast the elegant surfaces of society with the corruption that lies beneath. A classic scene is the first meeting between Monescu and Lily, two thieves with polished manners. In an elegant hotel room, the two engage in a genteel banter filled with seductive double-entendres and urbane banalities. But they are not the Baron and Countess they profess to be, as their behavior soon makes clear. As the supper progresses, they manage to steal one another's wallets, jewelry, and watches. Finally, they reveal the thefts to one another and sort out their belongings, but Monescu has been won over by Lily's cleverness, for he admires her resourcefulness far more than the undeserved wealth of the upper classes.

Lubitsch went on to make many more films during the 1930s, comedies of manners and musical comedies as well. Among his greatest Hollywood films are *Design for Living* (1933), *The Merry Widow* (1934), *Ninotchka* (1939), and *Heaven Can Wait* (1943). One of the wittiest directors of all time, he made films in English, German and French, always exhibiting the sharpest eye for detail. His films challenged the intellect of his viewers, and they never disappointed. The juxtaposition of seemingly contradictory elements was always central to his style, as he exposed the falsehoods he found in his world.

QUESTIONS

1. Which of the following terms would *not* be a good description of Lubitsch's film style, as it is described in the text?
   A. Sophisticated
   B. Erudite
   C. Chic
   D. Boisterous

2. One of the tools that Lubitsch used to mock the upper classes, as shown in the text, was
   F. Lighting.
   G. Talking pictures.
   H. Juxtaposition of contradictory elements.
   J. Urbane banalities.

3. Lubitsch's signature style can be described as
   A. Double-entendres and urbane banalities.
   B. Using apparently insignificant details as symbols.
   C. Charm and elegant manners.
   D. Corruption underlying high society.

4. Lubitsch first came to the U.S in 1923 because
   F. His films were not well received in Germany.
   G. He was fleeing the Nazi regime.
   H. He was invited by a producer.
   J. He could not make films with sound in Germany.

5. The text tells us that Lubitsch's first film, *Passion* was
   A. An early "talkie."
   B. A comedy of manners.
   C. A film starring Miriam Hopkins.
   D. None of the above.

6. Without considering gender, which two characters have the most in common?
    F. Monescu and Lily
    G. Monescu and Mariette
    H. Lily and Mariette
    J. Monescu and Lubitsch

7. The scene with the garbage gondola at the opening of the film shows that
    A. The rich need supporting services.
    B. Venice is kept clean by gondoliers.
    C. Elegance may be only a veneer.
    D. Gondoliers sing romantic ballads.

8. Monescu most admires
    F. Lily's wealth.
    G. Lily's cleverness.
    H. Mariette's money.
    J. Venetian gondolas.

9. In the film, Lily pretends to be
    A. A perfume heiress.
    B. A countess.
    C. A wealthy dowager.
    D. Monescu's partner.

10. In addition to the films he made in Hollywood and Germany, the text suggests that Lubitsch made movies in
    F. England.
    G. France.
    H. Spain.
    J. Lisbon.

Science Test

Part A.

Blood consists of a liquid called *plasma*, in which many different types of blood cells are suspended. The plasma also contains many dissolved proteins. These proteins may be studied by subjecting the plasma to *electrophoresis,* in which it is subjected to an electric field, which pulls the proteins through a porous gel. Proteins typically have a negative charge on their surface, so they move toward the anode (positive electrode) in an electric field. The gel acts as a molecular sieve: it interferes with the movement, or *migration*, of the larger proteins more than the small ones, allowing the proteins to be separated on the basis of size. The further the proteins move during the experiment, the smaller they must be.

The experiment results in an *electropherogram*, such as the one shown in the figure below. This is a plot, or graph, of protein concentration versus migration, and corresponds to a graph of concentration versus size. Concentration is measured by passing light of a certain wavelength through the gel: proteins absorb the light, and the resulting *absorbance* measurement is proportional to protein concentration. Many major blood component proteins, such as albumin and several identified by Greek letters, have been discovered in this way. When disease is present, some component proteins may break down into smaller fragments. Others may aggregate, or clump together, to form larger fragments. This results in a change in the electropherogram: new species, corresponding to the aggregates or breakdown products, may be present, and the sizes of the normal peaks may be changed as the concentration of normal products is altered.

The Figure shows an electropherogram from a sick patient with an abnormal component in her blood (arrow). Peaks corresponding to some normal plasma proteins have been labeled. Please examine the electropherogram and answer the following questions.

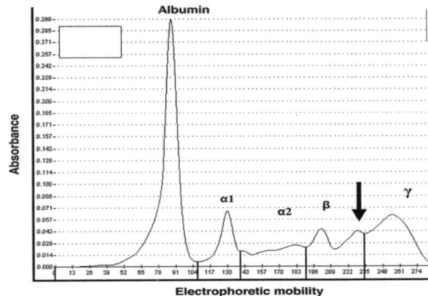

- 114 -

QUESTIONS:

1. Which blood component protein is present in the greatest amounts in the plasma?
   A. Albumin
   B. $\alpha 1$
   C. $\alpha 2$
   D. β

2. Which of the following is the fastest-moving component in the electropherogram?
   F. Albumin
   G. $\alpha 1$
   H. $\alpha 2$
   J. γ

3. Which of the following statements is true about component $\alpha 1$?
   A. The molecules move through the gel faster than those of component $\alpha 2$, but slower than Albumin.
   B. The molecules are larger than albumin, but smaller than all the other components.
   C. The molecules are smaller than albumin, but larger than all the other components.
   D. It is not a protein.

4. Which of the components identified on the electropherogram is the smallest molecule?
   F. Albumin
   G. $\alpha 1$
   H. $\alpha 2$
   J. γ

5. Which of the following is true of the unknown component identified by the arrow?
   A. The molecules are larger than the β component, but smaller than albumin
   B. The molecules are larger than the β component, but smaller than the γ component.
   C. The molecules move more slowly in the gel than all the other components except one.
   D. The molecules move more rapidly in the gel than all the other components except one.

6. Which of the following may be true of the unknown component identified by the arrow?
   F. It is formed of albumin molecules that have aggregated.
   G. It is formed of $\alpha 1$ molecules that have aggregated.
   H. It is formed of $\alpha 2$ molecules that have aggregated.
   J. It is formed of γ molecules that have aggregated.

7. Which of the following may not be true of the unknown component identified by the arrow?
   A. It is formed of albumin molecules that have broken down into fragments.
   B. It is formed of $\alpha 1$ molecules that have broken down into fragments.
   C. It is formed of $\alpha 2$ molecules that have broken down into fragments.
   D. It is formed of γ molecules that have broken down into fragments.

- 115 -

8. The blood of healthy individuals does not contain the unknown component indicated by the arrow. The experiment therefore proves

    F. The unknown component causes the patient's sickness.

    G. The unknown component results from the patient's sickness.

    H. The more of the unknown component there is, the sicker the patient will be.

    J. None of the above.

In a study performed to determine the migration patterns of fish, 34,000 juvenile sablefish of the species *Anoplopoma fimbria* were tagged and released into waters of the eastern Gulf of Alaska during a twenty-year period. The tagged fish were all juveniles (less than 2 years of age), so that the age of the recovered fish could be determined from the date on the tag. This allowed age-specific movement patterns to be studied. Tagged fish were recovered from sites in the Bering Sea, throughout the Gulf of Alaska, and off the coast of British Columbia. The fish were recovered by commercial fishermen, with the results reported to the scientists performing the study. A total of 2011 tagged fish were recovered. It was found that fish spawned in coastal waters move to deeper waters when they are older. At the same time, they migrate north and west, across the Gulf of Alaska toward the Aleutian Islands. Eventually, they return to the eastern Gulf as adults.

The figure shows tag recoveries from sablefish tagged as juveniles by age (in years) and by depth (in meters) for all the areas in the study. The size of each circle is proportional to the number of recoveries. The range for each data point is 1 to 57 recoveries. The symbol x represents the median age.

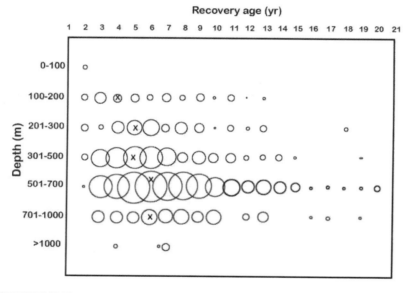

QUESTIONS:

9. If a circle in the graph is twice the size (area) of another circle, this indicates that:
   A. It represents twice as many fish.
   B. The fish it represents were twice as old.
   C. The fish it represents were recovered at twice the depth.
   D. Both A and B.

10. The greatest number of tagged fish were recovered at depths of
   F. 101 – 200 m.
   G. 201 – 300 m.
   H. 301 – 500 m.
   J. 501 – 700 m.

11. What percentage of the released, tagged fish were recovered for this study?
    A. 2011
    B. 20
    C. 6
    D. Can't determine from the data given.

12. The median age of tagged fish recovered at depths between 301 and 500 meters is approximately
    F. 2 years.
    G. 5 years.
    H. 9 years.
    J. Data not shown.

13. Not all the tagged fish were recovered in this study. Which of the following reasons may be responsible for the losses?
    A. Some fish died during the study.
    B. Some tagged fish were not caught by commercial fishermen during the study.
    C. The tags fell off some of the fish during the study.
    D. All of the above.

14. The largest fish are found at depths of
    F. 101 – 200 m.
    G. 201 – 300 m.
    H. 301 – 500 m.
    J. Can't determine from the data given.

15. Which of the following statements is supported by the data in the figure?
    A. Fish return to the eastern Gulf of Alaska to spawn.
    B. Sablefish move progressively deeper with age.
    C. Sablefish prefer cold waters.
    D. Younger fish swim faster than older ones.

16. The data indicate that sablefish may live as long as
    F. 10 years.
    G. 30 years.
    H. 20 years.
    J. 5 years.

Part C.

Pollutants typically enter seawater at *point sources*, such as sewage discharge pipes or factory waste outlets. Then, they may be spread over a wide area by wave action and currents. The rate of this dispersal depends upon a number of factors, including depth, temperature, and the speed of the currents. Chemical pollutants often attach themselves to small particles of sediment, so that studying the dispersal of sediment can help in understanding how pollution spreads.

In a study of this type, a team of scientists lowered screened collection vessels to various depths to collect particles of different sizes. This gave them an idea of the size distribution of particles at each depth. Figure A shows the results for six different sites (ND, NS, MD, MS, SD, and SS). The particle size is plotted in *phi* units, which is a logarithmic scale used to measure grain sizes of sand and gravel. The 0 point of the scale is a grain size of 1 millimeter, and an increase of 1 in phi number corresponds to a decrease in grain size by a factor of ½, so that 1 phi unit is a grain size of 0.5 mm, 2 phi units is 0.25 mm, and so on; in the other direction, -1 phi unit corresponds to a grain size of 2 mm and -2 phi units to 4 mm. Grains of different size are carried at different rates by the currents in the water. The study also measured current speed and direction, pressure and temperature at different depths, and at different times of year. The results were used in a computer *modeling program* to predict the total transport of sediments both along the shore (north-south) and perpendicular to it (east-west). Figure B shows the program's calculation of the distance particles would have been transported during the study period. The abbreviation *mab* in the figure stands for *meters above bottom*.

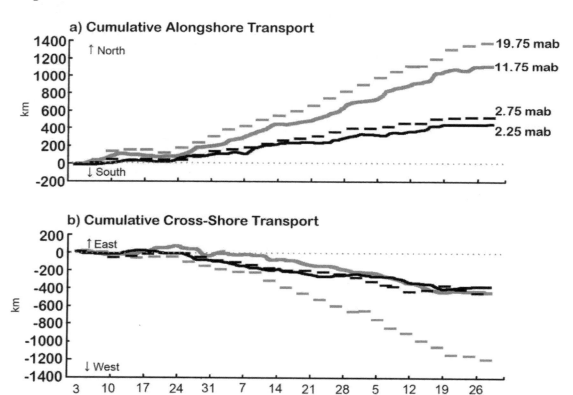

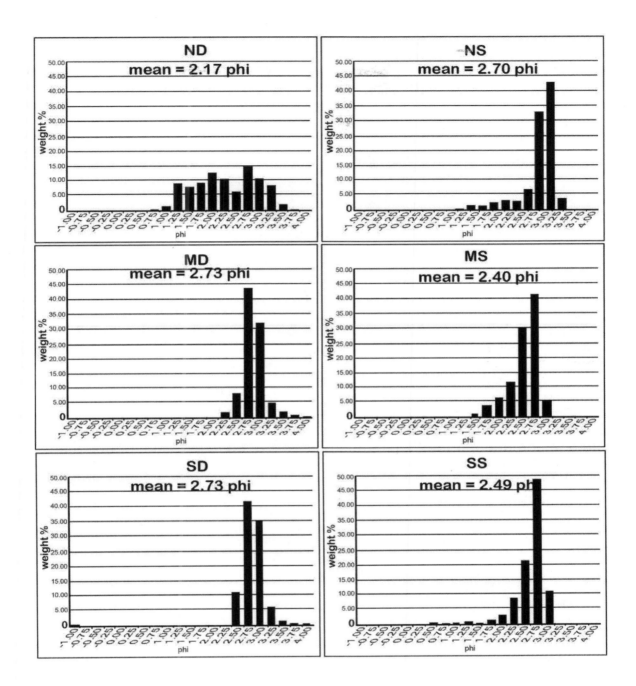

QUESTIONS:

17. Which of the following sites was found to have the smallest average particle size?
    A. ND
    B. NS
    C. MD
    D. MS

18. With the exception of a few outliers, all of the phi values were in the range 1.0 to 4.0. This means that
    F. All particles studied were smaller than 0.5 mm.
    G. All particles studied were between 1.0 and 4.0 mm.
    H. No screens larger than 4.0 m were used in the study.
    J. All particles were larger than 0.5 mm.

19. For which site is it least true that the mean particle size represents the entire population?
    A. ND
    B. NS
    C. MD
    D. MS

20. What particle size corresponds to a phi value of -3?
    F. 2mm
    G. 0.5 mm
    H. 0.0625 mm
    J. 8 mm

21. In Figure B, the absolute value of the slope of the curves corresponds to
    A. The speed of transport.
    B. The size of the particles.
    C. The phi value.
    D. The depth.

22. The data indicates that along a NS axis
    F. Transport is faster in deeper waters.
    G. Transport is faster in shallower waters.
    H. Transport is the same at all depths.
    J. There is no correlation between transport speed and depth.

23. The data indicates that along the EW axis
    A. Transport is faster in deeper waters.
    B. Transport is faster in shallower waters.
    C. Transport is the same at all depths.
    D. There is no correlation between transport speed and depth.

24. Which of the following is closest to the overall direction of transport?
    F. N
    G. NW
    H. NE
    J. SE

Part D.

Wind can provide a renewable source of energy. The energy of the wind is actually solar energy, as the sun warms the Earth's surface by varying amounts at different locations. This creates differential pressures as the warm air expands, and initiates air motions. High altitude airflows are similar to ocean currents, but near the surface, winds are affected by surface features.

Wind turbines capture this energy with a set of rotors that are set into rotation by the wind. The rotors are made of lightweight fiberglass or carbon fiber, and are held aloft on a tall tower. It is important to hold the blades high above the ground to avoid wind shear, a difference in airflow at different points along the rotor blades which can damage them. The blades rotate at about 40 rpm. Through a gearbox, they rotate a driveshaft at about 1500 rpm. The shaft, in turn, drives a generator.

The power P available from moving air is proportional to the cube of the wind velocity:

$$P = \frac{1}{2} \rho A v^3$$

where A is the cross section covered by the blades, ρ is the air density, and v is the air velocity. As the air passes through the rotor, it slows down. The turbine cannot take all the energy from the air, since then it would stop dead behind the rotor. Theoretically, the maximum efficiency that can be achieved is 59%. Figures A and B show a power curve for a 600 kilowatt (kW) wind turbine. To avoid damage from excessive winds, starting with wind speeds of 15 m/sec, the blades are adjusted to limit the power to 600 kW. For winds above 25 m/sec, the turbine is shut down.

One drawback of wind turbines has been the noise they make, but modern designs with slow-rotating blades are fairly quiet. Figure C shows the noise spectrum of a large turbine. The x-axis shows the frequency of sound in Hertz, and the y-axis shows the level of sound at each frequency. The total noise is 50 decibels (dB), which is less than the noise in a typical office.

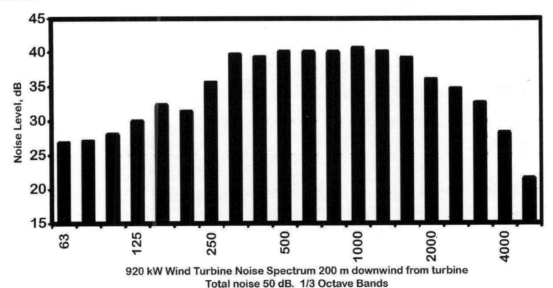

920 kW Wind Turbine Noise Spectrum 200 m downwind from turbine
Total noise 50 dB. 1/3 Octave Bands

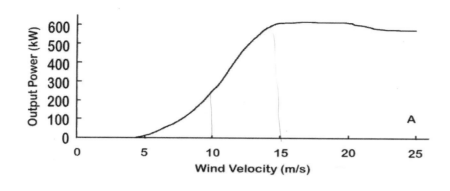

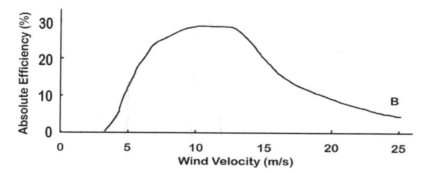

QUESTIONS:

25. What wind velocity provides the maximum efficiency for this turbine?
    A. 5 m/s
    B. 7 m/s
    C. 10 m/s
    D. 12 m/s

26. What wind velocity provides the maximum power output from this turbine?
    F. 5 m/s
    G. 7 m/s
    H. 10 m/s
    J. 15 m/s

27. Why does the curve in Figure A flatten for wind velocities greater than 15 m/sec?
    A. The generator runs less efficiently.
    B. The rotors are being trimmed to prevent damage.
    C. Surface turbulence makes the rotors turn more slowly.
    D. Wind shear makes the rotors turn more slowly.

28. For wind speeds between 5 and 10 m/sec, we expect the curve in Figure A to increase
    F. Linearly
    G. Irregularly
    H. Exponentially
    J. Sinusoidally

Answers and Explanations

English Test

Answer Key

PASSAGE I		PASSAGE II		PASSAGE III	
Question	Answer	Question	Answer	Question	Answer
1	C	1	C	1	A
2	J	2	H	2	G
3	B	3	C	3	C
4	G	4	J	4	G
5	B	5	B	5	C
6	F	6	F	6	F
7	A	7	B	7	D
8	G	8	H	8	H
9	B	9	D	9	C
10	G	10	G	10	G
11	D	11	B		
12	G	12	H		
13	C	13	D		
14	H	14	G		
15	C	15	D		

Answers: Passage I

1.   The best answer is C. In the original text, the word "would" is slang and adds nothing to the sentence. Answers B and D differ in meaning from the original.

2.   The best answer is J. The hyphens clarify the meaning by showing that the entire three-word clause modifies the expression "food supply."

3.   The best answer is B. By separating the modifying clause "in recent years," it clarifies the meaning of the sentence.

4.   The best answer is G. The original does not specify who is referred to by the word "their," which is unnecessary. Answer J is incorrect usage.

5.   The best answer is B. The word "that" has already appeared ("you would think that...") and is redundant if used again here.

6.   The best answer is F. None of the other spellings make sense in this usage.

7.   The best answer is A. The percentage plainly refers to the population mentioned earlier in the sentence. All the other answers are redundant.

8.   The best answer is G, which is the possessive of a plural noun. The original text offers the possessive of a singular noun, which is incorrect. The other answers are not possessives.

9.   The best answer is B, which is also the simplest. The word "still" in the original suggests that people will not buy expensive foods even if some other condition is met, but no such condition is specified. Therefore, the word is unnecessary and confusing.

10.   The best answer is G. The word "your" in the original is slang usage. Answer H is incorrect because it is a plural, not a possessive.

11.   The best answer is D. In this case, "too" means "also."

12.   The best answer is G. The phrase is redundant since the word "theory" is included in the name "the paycheck cycle theory" which follows immediately afterwards in the sentence.

13.   The best answer is C. The word "family" is used redundantly in the original sentence, and is easily replaced by a pronoun in this case.

14.   The best answer is H. The hypothesis suggests the *existence* of a cycle that promotes weight gain. In the original, the word "that" makes the sentence nonsensical.

15.   The best answer is C. The use of "would" in the original is slang. The author is saying that, if the paycheck cycle hypothesis is correct, the two causes of overweight are periodic food restriction and poor diet. Since there is some uncertainty here, C is a better choice than B.

Answers: Passage II

1. The best answer is C, which is the possessive of the plural noun "women."

2. The best answer is H, which is a possessive. Answer J is technically correct, but it is common usage to use this expression as a collective noun, so that "porter's lodge" can describe a lodge for more than one porter.

3. The correct answer is C. The other answers do not make sense.

4. The best answer is J. The original text's "accesses" requires a singular subject.

5. The best answer is B. Answer C changes the meaning, suggesting that the action is not performed every day, whereas the original text indicates that it occurs daily but that the time is indefinite.

6. The best answer is F. "Entryway" is the correct spelling.

7. The best answer is B. The phrase in the original is unnecessary, and is redundant as it repeats "only." The other answers are unnecessarily wordy.

8. The best answer is H. The original text splits the infinitive "to receive." Answers G and J imply that this happens all the time, whereas the text implies that it is an exceptional occurrence.

9. The best answer is D. Answer C repeats the word "even" and is redundant.

10. The best answer is G. The original text is phrased awkwardly, and answers H and J change the meaning.

11. The best answer is B. This provides a parallel construction between "morning" and "evening."

12. The best answer is H. The original seeks to imply that the guards are not effectively on watch, but the phrasing is awkward and makes no sense. Answer G is correctly spelled, but retains the awkward phrasing of the original.

13. The best answer is D. Since all the elements of the list contain verbs, this choice provides for parallel construction by also including the verb. Answer C is less desirable since the phrase "physically out of shape" is redundant.

14. The best answer is G. The other choices are unnecessarily wordy.

15. The best answer is D, which most specifically explains what has been ineffective about the tactics of the guards. Answer C is vague.

Answers: Passage III

1.   The best answer is A. Capitalization is required since the school name is a proper noun, and a possessive is needed since the program belongs to the school.

2.   The best answer is G. The infinitive ("to do") should always be used in the present tense.

3.   The best answer is C. The infinitive ("to afford") should always be used in the present tense.

4.   The best answer is G. The original is redundant, since "at last" and "finally" have the same meaning.

5.   The best answer is C. The original version is awkward, since it repeats the word "soon" which appeared earlier in the same sentence.

6.   The best answer is F. The comma is not required before a subordinating conjunction such as "until."

7.   The best answer is D. The commas are used to set off Dr. Ed Cook's name as a parenthetical element.

8.   The best answer is H. In the original version, the word "this" is slang usage.

9.   The best answer is C. The original version is nonsensical, and none of the other answers are grammatically correct.

10.   The best answer is G. Answer H is grammatically correct, but the phrase adds nothing to the author's description of the purpose of the work done on board the boat.

Mathematics Test

1. The correct answer is D. An easy way to do this is to remember that for a number to be divisible by 3, the sum of the digits must be divisible by 3. Thus, for 555, 5+5+5=15, and 15/3 = 5. 555/3 = 185

A. 2+0+1+8 = 11, which is not divisible by 3.

B. 4+6 = 10, which is not divisible by 3.

C. 8+9+1+2=20, which is not divisible by 3.

E. 7+3+9 = 19, which is not divisible by 3.

2. The correct answer is G. 25% off is equivalent to $25 \times \dfrac{\$138}{100} = \$34.50$, so the sale price becomes \$138 - \$34.50 = \$103.50.

F. $\$67 \neq \$103.50$

H. \$34.50 is the amount of the reduction, not the final price.

J. $\$113 \neq \$103.50$

K. $\$125 \neq 103.50$

3. The correct answer is C. The expression 2^{-3} is equivalent to $\dfrac{1}{2^3}$, and since $2^3 = 8$, it is equivalent to 1/8.

A. $\dfrac{1}{4} = 2^{-2}$

B. $\dfrac{1}{12} \neq \dfrac{1}{8}$

D. $\dfrac{1}{16} = 2^{-4}$

E. $\dfrac{1}{12} \neq \dfrac{1}{8}$

4. The correct answer is G. 30% 0f 3300 = 0.3 x 3300 = 990

F. 330 is $\dfrac{330}{3300} \times 100 = 10\%$ of 3300, not 30%

H. 700 is $\dfrac{700}{3300} \times 100 = 21.2\%$ of 3300, not 30%

J. 1100 is $\dfrac{1100}{3300} \times 100 = 33.3\%$ of 3300, not 30%

K. 2310 is $\dfrac{2310}{3310} \times 100 = 70\%$ of 3300, not 30%

5. The correct answer is B. The value of the fraction $\dfrac{7}{5}$ can be evaluated by dividing 7 by 5, which yields 1.4. The average of 1.4 and 1.4 is $\dfrac{1.4 + 1.4}{2} = 1.4$.

Answers A, C, and D are incorrect because the solution to a numeric equation is unique. E is incorrect because B provides the correct answer.

- 128 -

6. The correct answer is H.
The surface of a cube is obtained by multiplying the area of each face by 6, since there are 6 faces. The area of each face is the square of the length of one edge. Therefore
$A = 6 \times 3^2 = 6 \times 9 = 54$.
Answers F, G, J, and K are incorrect since the surface area is a unique value.

7. The correct answer is D. Inspection of the data shows that the distance traveled by the car during any 1-unit interval (velocity) is 20 units. However, the first data point shows that the car is 50 units from the point of origin at time 2, so it had a 10-unit head start before time measurement began.
Answers A-C only fit the data at single points. They do not fit the whole set.
Answer E is incorrect since answer D fits all the data.

8. The correct answer is H. The total distance traveled was 8 + 3.6 = 11.6 miles. The first $1/5^{th}$ of a mile is charged at the higher rate. Since $1/5^{th}$ = 0.2, the remainder of the trip is 11.4 miles. Thus the fare for the distance traveled is computed as
$\$5.50 + 5 \times 11.4 \times \$1.50 = \$91$. To this the charge for waiting time must be added, which is simply 9 x 20¢ = 180¢ = $1.80. Finally, add the two charges, $91 + $1.80 = $92.80.
Since this value is unique, all other answers are incorrect.

9. The correct answer is E. Each term of each expression in parentheses must be multiplied by each term in the other. Thus for E, $(x+3)(3x-5) = 3x^2 + 9x - 5x - 15 = 3x^2 + 4x - 15$
A. $(x-3)(x+5) = x^2 - 3x + 5x - 15 = x^2 + 2x - 15 \neq 3x^2 + 4x - 15$
B. $(x+5)(3+x^2) = 3x + 15 + x^3 + 5x^2 \neq 3x^2 + 4x - 15$
C. $x(3x + 4 - 15) = 3x^2 + 4x - 15x = 3x^2 - 11x \neq 3x^2 + 4x - 15$
D. $(3x^2 + 5)(3x - 5) = (9x^3 + 15x - 5x^2 - 25) \neq 3x^2 + 4x - 15$

10. The correct answer is G. First determine the proportion of students in Grade 5. Since the total number of students is 180, this proportion is $\frac{36}{180} = 0.2$, or 20%. Then determine the same proportion of the total prizes, which is 20% of twenty, or $0.2 \times 20 = 4$.
F. $5 \neq 0.2 \times 20$
H. $7 \neq 0.2 \times 20$
J. $3 \neq 0.2 \times 20$
K. $2 \neq 0.2 \times 20$

11. The correct answer is B. The probability of playing a song by any band is proportional to the number of songs by that band over the total number of songs, or $\frac{5}{15} = \frac{1}{3}$ for Band D.
The probability of playing any particular song is not affected by what has been played previously, since the choice is random.
Since this value is unique, answers A, C, and D are incorrect.
E. is incorrect since the answer can be computed as shown.

12. The correct answer is F. Since 3 of the 15 songs are by Band B, the probability that any one song will be by that band is $\frac{3}{15} = \frac{1}{5}$. The probability that two successive events will occur is the product of the probabilities for any one event or, in this case $\frac{1}{5} \times \frac{1}{5} = \frac{1}{25}$.
Since this value is unique, answers G, H, and J are incorrect.
K. is incorrect since the answer can be computed as shown.

13. The correct answer is B. A prime number is a natural, positive, non-zero number which can be factored only by itself and by 1. This is the case for 11.
A. 15 = 5 x 3, and thus is not a prime number.
C. 33 = 11 x 3, and thus is not a prime number.
D. 4 = 2 x 2, and thus is not a prime number.
E. 88 = 11 x 8 (among many other factoring possibilities) , and thus is not a prime number.

14. The correct answer is G. Compute as follows: $(3-2 \times 2)^2 = (3-4)^2 = (-1)^2 = 1.$
H is incorrect since $4 \neq 2$.
All other answers are incorrect since they are negative, and the squared expression must be greater than 0.

15. The correct answer is A. Each glass of lemonade costs 10¢, or $0.10, so that g glasses will cost $0.10*g. To this, add Bob's fixed cost of $45, giving the expression in A.
$44.90*g ≠ $45 + $0.10*g
$44.90*g+$0.10 ≠ $45 + $0.10*g
$90 ≠ $45 + $0.10*g
$45.10 ≠ $45 + $0.10*g

16. The correct answer is G. The lowest score, 68, is eliminated. The average of the remaining four grades is

$$Avg = \frac{75 + 88 + 86 + 90}{4} = 84.75$$

Rounding up to the nearest integer gives a final grade of 85. Since this value is unique, all the other answers are incorrect.

17. The correct answer is B. To calculate S, calculate the discount and subtract it from the original price, p. The discount is 33% of p, or 0.33p. Thus, $S = p - 0.33p$.

A. $S = p - 0.33 \neq$ p-0.33p
C. $S = 0.33p \neq$ p-0.33p
D. $S = 0.33(1-p) \neq$ p-0.33p
E. $S = p + 0.33p \neq$ p-0.33p

18. The correct answer is F. The band's share, 25% of $20,000,000, is $5,000,000. After the agent's share is subtracted, the band gets
$(1-0.15) \times \$5,000,000 = 0.85 \times \$5,000,000 = \$4,250,000$
and each band member gets one fifth of that, or $850,000.
Since this value is unique, all the other answers are incorrect.

19. The correct answer is C. Rearranging the equation gives
$3(x+4)=15(x-5)$, which is equivalent to
$15x-3x=12+75$, or
$12x=87$, and solving for x,
$$x=\frac{87}{12}=\frac{29}{4}.$$
Since this value is unique, all the other answers are incorrect.

20. The correct answer is G. The median is the value in a group of numbers that separates the upper half from the lower half, so that there are an equal number of values above and below it. In this distribution, there are two values greater than 116, and two values below it.
F. is the mean, or average of the distribution, not the median.
H. is the most common value, or mode of the distribution, not the median.
J and K are simply values within the range of the distribution. They are not the median.

21. The correct answer is B. $7.5 \times 10^{-4} = \dfrac{7.5}{10,000} = 0.00075$
Since this value is unique, all the other answers are incorrect.

22. The correct answer is F. Rearranging the equation gives $x^2 = -1$. However, the square of a real number cannot yield a negative result, so no real number solutions exist for the equation.
Answers G-K are incorrect, since it has been shown that there are no real number solutions.

23. B: Any color can be drawn the first time, leaving five marbles. At this point, only one of the five is the same color as the one that was drawn the fist time. The odds of selecting this marble are one chance in five, or 20%.

24. G: The reciprocal of 5 is $\dfrac{1}{5}$. When numbers are multiplied by their reciprocals, the result is always 1. Thus, $5 \times \dfrac{1}{5} = 1$.

25. A: Negative numbers represent segments extending to the left of zero on the number line. Adding a negative number to another negative number extends the segment even further to the left, or into "negative territory". To add two negative numbers, add the magnitudes and retain the negative sign. For example
(-3) + (-5) = -8.

26. F: An odd number can be considered as an even number N plus 1. Two even numbers added together produce an even number, so the result of adding an odd and an even number must be an even number plus 1, which is odd. For example, 4 + 3 = 7.

27. C: At 10%, Richard is paid $\$140 \times 10\% = \dfrac{10(140)}{100} = \$14$ for every phone he sells. To make $840, he must sell $\dfrac{840}{14} = 60$ phones.

28. G: If x represents the width of the box, its length is equal to $2x$. Since the sides of a square are equal, $2x - 3 = x + 3$, and $x = 6$. So the box is 6 inches wide.

29. C: Since $11 - 5 = 6$, then $3x = 6$, and $x = \dfrac{6}{3} = 2$.

30. F: Each number in the list is 4 less than the number that precedes it, which means that 5 appropriately follows 9.

Reading Test

Prose Fict		Soc Sci		Humanity	
Question	Answer	Question	Answer	Question	Answer
1	C	1	B	1	D
2	G	2	G	2	H
3	B	3	C	3	B
4	J	4	H	4	H
5	C	5	B	5	D
6	G	6	H	6	F
7	A	7	B	7	C
8	F	8	H	8	G
9	D	9	B	9	B
10	G	10	F	10	G

Prose Fiction

1. The correct answer is C. The passage makes no mention of metals or horses. Although we may infer that they hunted the buffalo because they were plentiful, that is not stated in the passage.

2. The correct answer is G. Travail means work, or effort, and shows that the crows made it more difficult for the people to kill buffalo during the hunt.

3. The correct answer is B. The story tells us that after the great white crow turned black, all the other crows were black as well. Thus, he is a symbol for all these birds.

4. The correct answer is J. Line 18 tells us that the tribe planned to frighten the chief of the crows to prevent the crows from warning the buffalo about the hunts. The passage does not suggest that they hated all birds or that they planned to eat this one.

5. The correct answer is C. Long Arrow acted like the buffalo in the herd so that the chief of the crows would approach, making it possible to capture him. Although we may infer that he had to fool the buffalo in the herd as well, this is secondary to his need to fool the birds.

6. The correct answer is G. These details help us to see how the people lived. Although they hunted with the stone-tipped spears, the rawhide bag was not a part of the hunt.

7. The correct answer is A. As he lands, he asks "have you not heard my warning?" (Line 41).

8. The correct answer is F. The suggestions included several for killing or mutilating the bird, which does not suggest a calm resolve. And there is no suggestion that they were either celebrating or hungry at this time.

9. The correct answer is D. There is no characterization of Long Arrow in the passage, and we know nothing about him or why he was chosen.

10. The correct answer is G. The birds in the story are able to observe the actions of hunters, to interpret them as potentially harmful for their buffalo friends, and to act for the protection of the buffalo. They do not appear to do this for their own benefit, nor do they seem to act specifically to harm the tribe, but rather to help the buffalo.

Social Science
1. The correct answer is B. The first paragraph refers to the Spray as a sloop, which is a kind of sailboat, and refers to its being berthed among the docks.

2. The correct answer is G. In the first paragraph the author describes his surprise at the changes in the harbor, and in Lines 8-10 indicates that the changes downtown were much less.

3. The correct answer is C. Lines 10 mentions a letter of introduction that had been sent ahead from another of the author's contacts in Montevideo.

4. The correct answer is H. Line 15 mentions the "Standard's" columns, which had contained stories about the Spray's voyage.

5. The correct answer is B. Although "landmarks" are usually monuments or buildings, the author uses the term and goes on to describe a number of merchants who had been present during his earlier visit to the city, and who were significant features of the town in his estimation.

6. The correct answer is H. Line 22 tells us that the lemons "went on forever," suggesting that the merchant hardly ever changed them at all.

7. The correct answer is B. The author would have liked to look up the whiskey merchant, but there is nothing in the passage to suggest that he was desperate or anxious to do so.

8. The correct answer is H. The phrase in Line 32, that the waters were not blameless of disease germs, indicates that some germs may have been present in them.

9. The correct answer is B. Throughout the passage, the author is looking for people he had seen on his first visit, and he says of this merchant that he had "survived" (Line 35).

10. The correct answer is F. Since the sign has been present since the author's previous visit to the city, we may infer that the merchant is not really concerned about an imminent comet strike. And the wording of the sign suggests that his wares are for sale "at any price" (Line 37).

Humanities

1. The correct answer is D. Choices A-C all have similar meanings and match the text's description of Lubitsch's film style as elegant or sophisticated.

2. The correct answer is H. This phrase is used in the last sentence to describe the Lubitsch style.

3. The correct answer is B. Lubitsch's focus on seemingly irrelevant details as symbols is described in the text as his signature style (Line 14)

4. The correct answer is H. Lubitsch was invited in 1923 by Albert Zukor (Line 12).

5. The correct answer is D. Made in 1912, the film could not have been a talkie, as it was not until 1923 that Lubitsch went to Hollywood to use sound technology. And the text tells us nothing of the film's content or personnel.

6. The correct answer is F. Monescu and Lily were both thieves who posed as members of high society. Mariette was a real heiress, and Lubitsch, of course, was a director, not a character in the film.

7. The correct answer is C. This, indeed, is the underlying theme of the entire movie, as shown by the characters of Monescu and Lily, who appear to be elegant but are, in fact, thieves.

8. The correct answer is G. Lily has no wealth of her own, but Monescu finally chooses her over Mariette and her fortune (Lines 42-43)

9. The correct answer is B. Lily passes herself of as a countess and Montescu poses as a baron (Line 39).

10. The correct answer is G. Line 49 tells us that he made films in English, German, and French, suggesting that part of his film career was spent in France.

- 135 -

Science Test

PART A		PART B		PART C		PART D	
Q	A	Q	A	Q	A	Q	A
1	A	9	A	17	C	25	C
2	J	10	J	18	J	26	J
3	C	11	C	19	A	27	B
4	J	12	G	20	J	28	H
5	D	13	D	21	A		
6	J	14	J	22	G		
7	D	15	B	23	B		
8	J	16	H	24	G		

1. The correct answer is A. The peak for albumin is the highest in the electropherogram, so the concentration of albumin is higher than that of any other component.
Answers B-D are incorrect, since all the corresponding peaks are lower.

2. The correct answer is J. The peak for component γ is furthest from the origin along the mobility axis, indicating that it has moved the furthest during the experiment.
Answers F-H are incorrect, since the corresponding peaks are further to the left, indicating lesser mobility for these components.

3. The correct answer is C. The peak for component $\alpha 1$ lies to the right of that for albumin, indicating greater mobility, and to the right of all the other peaks, indicating lesser mobility than the components represented by those peaks. Since small molecules move faster than large ones, $\alpha 1$ must be smaller than albumin and larger than the other components.
Answer A is incorrect because the peak for $\alpha 1$ is to the right (faster) than albumin and to the left (slower) than the others.
Answer B is incorrect because the peak for $\alpha 1$ is to the right (smaller) than albumin and to the left (larger) than the others.
Answer D is incorrect because the data say nothing about whether or not the component is a protein.

4. The correct answer is J. The peak for component γ is the fastest, indicating that γ is the smallest component seen on the electropherogram.
Answers F-H are incorrect because all these components move more slowly than component γ.

5. The correct answer is D. The peak for the unknown lies between those for γ and β, indicating an intermediate size. It has moved more rapidly than all components except for component γ.

Answers A and B are incorrect, because the unknown is smaller than β
Answer C is incorrect, because the unknown is faster than most of the others,

6. The correct answer is J. If the unknown is an aggregate, it must be larger than the components that have clumped together to form it, not smaller. Answers F-H are incorrect, because the components they refer to are all larger than the unknown, so they cannot form it by aggregation.

7. The correct answer is D. If the unknown is a breakdown product, it must be smaller than the components that have broken down to form it, not larger. Answers A-C are incorrect, because the components they refer to are all larger than the unknown, so it <u>may</u> be true that any of these have formed it by breaking down.

8. The correct answer is J. The experiment shows only that this patient's blood contains an unknown component. It does not demonstrate that the component causes the patient's disease, or that it results from it. It may be unrelated. Further experiments are required to fully characterize the relationship between the component and the illness.
Answers F-H are incorrect because all assume a cause-and-effect relationship between the component and the patient's illness, but this has not been demonstrated by this one experiment.

9. The correct answer is A. As stated in the text, the size of each circle is proportional to the number of recoveries.

10. The correct answer is J. The graph shows that the largest number of circles, and the largest circles as well, are at this depth. Since the size of the circles is proportional to the number of fish recovered, the greatest numbers of these fish were at these depths.

11. The correct answer is C. 2011 fish were recovered out of 34,000 released. The percentage is given by $P = 100 \times \dfrac{2{,}011}{34{,}000} = 6\%$.

12. The correct answer is G. The median age at each depth is shown by the X symbols on the plot. For this depth, the symbol lines up approximately with the mark corresponding to 5 years on the upper axis of the graph.

13. The correct answer is D. Although not specifically described in the text, all of the reasons stated may occur, reducing the recovery of tagged fish. The conclusions of the study must assume that the fraction of fish recovered (sample) are representative of the population as a whole.

14. The correct answer is J. The chart describes the age of the fish, but does not provide any information concerning their size.

15. The correct answer is B. The median age of the populations recovered at each depth is shown by the X symbol on the plot, and corresponds to progressively older fish at greater

depths. Although some of the other statements are true, they are not supported by the data in the figure.

16. The correct answer is H. The right-most symbol on the plot shows that some 20-year old fish were recovered at depths of 501-700 meters. No older fish were recovered in this study.

17. The correct answer is C. Of the sites listed, the phi value for site MD, 2.73 phi, is the largest value. The text explains how phi varies inversely with particle size, so these are the smallest particles.

18. The correct answer is J. According to the definition of phi supplied in the text, the range 1.0 to 4.0 phi units corresponds to particle sizes in the range 0.06 to 0.5 mm.

19. The correct answer is A. At all of the sites except site ND, the particle size distributions are tightly centered around a well-defined modal value. At site ND, the distribution is spread out over a broader range, and there is no well-defined central value.

20. The correct answer is J. Each unit of added phi value in the negative direction corresponds to a doubling of the particle size, so that -1 corresponds to 2mm, -2 to 4 mm, and -3 to 8 mm.

21. The correct answer is A. The curves represent the distance traveled, and they approximate a straight line. The slope of the line represents the speed of travel. Although the curve in part (b) has a negative slope, the absolute value of that slope will be a positive value, representing speed of transport towards the west.

22. The correct answer is G. The steepest slopes correspond to the greatest values of *mab*, or meters above bottom. These are the shallowest waters.

23. The correct answer is B. The steepest slopes correspond to the greatest values of *mab*, or meters above bottom. These are the shallowest waters. Although the slopes are negative in this plot, it is the magnitude of the slope that indicates the speed of transport. Here, the negative value simply indicates that the sediments drift toward the west, not the east.

24. The correct answer is G. The upper graph shows transport toward the north. The lower graph shows transport toward the west. If these two are combined, overall transport will be toward the NW.

25. The correct answer is C. The efficiency curve in part B of the figure has a clear maximum value at a wind velocity of 10 m/s.

26. The correct answer is J. The power curve in part A of the figure increases with increasing wind velocity, until a plateau is reached at 15 m/s and above.

27. The correct answer is B. The text explains that for wind velocities above 15 m/s, the rotor blades are trimmed to protect the equipment. Above 25 m/s, the turbine must be shut down.

28. The correct answer is H. Power increases with the cube of wind velocity. This is an exponential function.

Secret Key #1 – Time Is Your Greatest Enemy

To succeed on the EXPLORE you must use your time wisely. Most students do not finish at least one section.

Time constraints are brutal. To succeed, you must ration your time properly.

On every section except the Math, the test is separated into passages. The reason that time is so critical is that 1) every question counts the same toward your final score, and 2) the passages are not in order of difficulty. If you have to rush during the last passage, then you will miss out on answering easier questions correctly. It is natural to want to pause and figure out the hardest questions, but you must resist the temptation and move quickly.

Success Strategy #1

Wear a watch to the EXPLORE Test. At the beginning of the test, check the time (or start a chronometer on your watch to count the minutes), and check the time after each passage to make sure you are "on schedule."

SECTION	Time	# Questions
English	30 min	40
Reading	30 min	30
Science	30 min	28
Math	30 min	30

These limits are designed with a built-in "buffer" to make sure you have time left over to make final guesses and adjustments.

If you find that you are behind time during the test, work through the next passage more quickly. If you are still behind time after the next passage, skip the last question of the following passage in an attempt to catch up (unless you know it at a quick glance). Once you are caught up, maintain that pace until the end of the test.

The Math Section is the easiest to keep time on; move on if you take more than a minute on a question. Since the questions are pretty much in order of difficulty, if you have time left over, come back to the earliest skipped questions, spend another minute at most, and then move on to the next skipped question.

Always mark skipped questions in your workbook,. Last minute guessing will be covered in the next chapter.

The Reading section poses the greatest challenge for time-. Unless you are an uncommonly fast reader, I strongly suggest you follow our advice in the Reading Section covered later in the guide- focus on the questions, and scan for answers as necessary.

Lastly, sometimes it is beneficial to slow down if you are constantly getting ahead of time. You are always more likely to catch a careless mistake by working more slowly than quickly, and among very high-scoring students (those who are likely to have lots of time left over), careless errors affect the score more than mastery of material.

Secret Key #2 – Guessing is not Guesswork

You probably know that guessing is a good idea on the EXPLORE there is no penalty for getting a wrong answer. Even if you have no idea about a question, you still have a 20-25% chance of getting it right. Unless you score above 30 or so, guessing will contribute about 3-4 points to your final score.

Monkeys Take the EXPLORE

What most students don't realize is that to insure that 20-25% chance, you have to guess randomly. If you put 20 monkeys in a room to take the EXPLORE, assuming they answered once per question and behaved themselves, on average they would get 20-25% of the questions correct. Put 20 high school students in the room, and the average will be much lower among guessed questions. Why?

1. EXPLORE intentionally writes deceptive answer choices that "look" right. A student has no idea about a question, so picks the "best looking" answer, which is often wrong. The monkey has no idea what looks good and what doesn't, so will consistently be lucky about 20-25% of the time.
2. Students will eliminate answer choices from the guessing pool based on a hunch or intuition. Simple but correct answers often get excluded, leaving a 0% chance of being correct. The monkey has no clue, and often gets lucky with the best choice.

This is why the process of elimination endorsed by most test courses is flawed and detrimental to your performance- students don't guess, they make an ignorant stab in the dark that is usually worse than random.

Success Strategy #2

Let me introduce one of the most valuable ideas of this course- the $5 challenge:

You only mark your "best guess" if you are willing to bet $5 on it.

You only eliminate choices from guessing if you are willing to bet $5 on it.

Why $5? Five dollars is an amount of money that is small yet not insignificant, and can really add up fast (20 questions could cost you $100). Likewise, each answer choice on one question of the EXPLORE will have a small impact on your overall score, but it can really add up to a lot of points in the end.

The process of elimination IS valuable. The following shows your chance of guessing it right:

If you eliminate this many choices:	0	1	2	3	4
Math (5 choices)	20%	25%	33%	50%	100%
English / Reading / Science (4 choices)	25%	33%	50%	100%	N/A

However, if you accidentally eliminate the right answer or go on a hunch for an incorrect answer, your chances drop dramatically: to 0%. By guessing among all the answer choices, you are GUARANTEED to have a shot at the right answer.

That's why the $5 test is so valuable- if you give up the advantage and safety of a pure guess, it had better be worth the risk.

What we still haven't covered is how to be sure that whatever guess you make is truly random. Here's the easiest way:

Always pick the first answer choice among those remaining.

Such a technique means that you have decided, **before you see a single test question**, exactly how you are going to guess- and since the order of choices tells you nothing about which one is correct, this guessing technique is perfectly random.

Let's try an example-

A student encounters the following problem on the math test:

What is the cosine of an angle in a right triangle that is 3 meters on the adjacent side, 5 meters on the hypotenuse, and 4 meters on the opposite side?

A. 1
B. 0.6
C. 0.8
D. 0.75
E. 1.25

The student has a small idea about this question- he is pretty sure that cosine is opposite over hypotenuse, but he wouldn't bet $5 on it. He knows that cosine is "something" over hypotenuse, and since the hypotenuse is the largest number, he is willing to bet $5 on both choices A and E not being correct. So he is down to B, C, and D. At this point, he guesses B, since B is the first choice remaining.

The student is correct by choosing B, since cosine is adjacent over hypotenuse. He only eliminated those choices he was willing to bet money on, AND he did not let his stale memories (often things not known definitely will get mixed up in the exact opposite arrangement in one's head) about the formula for cosine influence his guess. He blindly chose the first remaining choice, and was rewarded with the fruits of a random guess.

This section is not meant to scare you away from making educated guesses or eliminating choices- you just need to define when a choice is worth eliminating. The $5 test, along with a pre-defined random guessing strategy, is the best way to make sure you reap all of the benefits of guessing.

Secret Key #3 – Practice Smarter, Not Harder

Many students delay the test preparation process because they dread the awful amounts of practice time they think necessary to succeed on the test. We have refined an effective method that will take you only a fraction of the time.

There are a number of "obstacles" in your way on the EXPLORE. Among these are answering questions, finishing in time, and mastering test-taking strategies. All must be executed on the day of the test at peak performance, or your score will suffer. The EXPLORE is a mental marathon.

Just like a marathon runner, it is important to work your way up to the full challenge. So first you just worry about questions, and then time, and finally strategy:

Success Strategy #3

1. Find a good source for EXPLORE practice tests. The best source for these will be the current and past "practice/registration packets" from EXPLORE. Your guidance counselor can provide you with the current one, and, if you're lucky, they may have a supply of old ones as well. You will need at least 3 practice tests.

2. If you are willing to make a larger time investment, consider using more than one study guide- often the different approaches of multiple authors will help you "get" difficult concepts.

3. Take a practice test with no time constraints, with all study helps "open book." Take your time with questions and focus on applying the strategies.

4. Take another test, this time with time constraints, with all guides "open book."

5. Take a final practice test with no open material and time limits.

If you have time to take more practice tests, just repeat step 5. By gradually exposing yourself to the full rigors of the test environment, you will condition your mind to the stress of test day and maximize your success.

Secret Key #4 – Make EXPLORE Work for You

Let me state an obvious fact: if you take The EXPLORE three times, you will get three different scores. This is due to the way you feel on test day, the level of preparedness you have, and, despite EXPLORE's claims to the contrary, some tests WILL be easier for you than others, especially on the "sectionized" English, Reading and Science tests.

Since your acceptance and qualification for scholarships will largely depend on your score, you should maximize your chances of success by taking The EXPLORE at least twice . We recommend taking The EXPLORE three times to fully account for all variances in performance, preparedness, and test difficulty.

Secret Key #5 - Test Yourself

Everyone knows that time is money. There is no need to spend too much of your time or too little of your time preparing for the test. You should only spend as much of your precious time preparing as is necessary for you to pass it.

Once you have taken a practice test under real conditions of time constraints, then you will know if you are ready for the test or not.

If you have scored extremely high the first time that you take the practice test, then there is not much point in spending countless hours studying. You are already there.

Benchmark your abilities by retaking practice tests and seeing how much you have improved. Once you score high enough to guarantee success, then you are ready.

If you have scored well below where you need, then knuckle down and begin studying in earnest. Check your improvement regularly through the use of practice tests under real conditions. Above all, don't worry, panic, or give up. The key is perseverance!

Then, when you go to take the test, remain confident and remember how well you did on the practice tests. If you can score high enough on a practice test, then you can do the same on the real thing.

General Strategies

The most important thing you can do is to ignore your fears and jump into the test immediately- do not be overwhelmed by any strange-sounding terms. You have to jump into the test like jumping into a pool- all at once is the easiest way.

Make Predictions

As you read and understand the question, try to guess what the answer will be. Remember that several of the answer choices are wrong, and once you begin reading them, your mind will immediately become cluttered with answer choices designed to throw you off. Your mind is typically the most focused immediately after you have read the question and digested its contents. If you can, try to predict what the correct answer will be. You may be surprised at what you can predict.

Quickly scan the choices and see if your prediction is in the listed answer choices. If it is, then you can be quite confident that you have the right answer. It still won't hurt to check the other answer choices, but most of the time, you've got it!

Answer the Question

It may seem obvious to only pick answer choices that answer the question, but the test writers can create some excellent answer choices that are wrong. Don't pick an answer just because it sounds right, or you believe it to be true. It MUST answer the question. Once you've made your selection, always go back and check it against the question and make sure that you didn't misread the question, and the answer choice does answer the question posed.

Benchmark

After you read the first answer choice, decide if you think it sounds correct or not. If it doesn't, move on to the next answer choice. If it does, mentally mark that answer choice. This doesn't mean that you've definitely selected it as your answer choice, it just means that it's the best you've seen thus far. Go ahead and read the next choice. If the next choice is worse than the one you've already selected, keep going to the next answer choice. If the next choice is better than the choice you've already selected, mentally mark the new answer choice as your best guess.

The first answer choice that you select becomes your standard. Every other answer choice must be benchmarked against that standard. That choice is correct until proven otherwise by another answer choice beating it out. Once you've decided that no other answer choice seems as good, do one final check to ensure that your answer choice answers the question posed.

Valid Information

Don't discount any of the information provided in the question. Every piece of information may be necessary to determine the correct answer. None of the information in the question is there to throw you off (while the answer choices will certainly have information to throw you off). If two seemingly unrelated topics are discussed, don't ignore either. You can be confident there is a relationship, or it wouldn't be included in the question, and you are probably going to have to determine what is that relationship to find the answer.

Avoid "Fact Traps"

Don't get distracted by a choice that is factually true. Your search is for the answer that answers the question. Stay focused and don't fall for an answer that is true but incorrect. Always go back to the question and make sure you're choosing an answer that actually answers the question and is not just a true statement. An answer can be factually correct, but it MUST answer the question asked. Additionally, two answers can both be seemingly correct, so be sure to read all of the answer choices, and make sure that you get the one that BEST answers the question.

Milk the Question

Some of the questions may throw you completely off. They might deal with a subject you have not been exposed to, or one that you haven't reviewed in years. While your lack of knowledge about the subject will be a hindrance, the question itself can give you many clues that will help you find the correct answer. Read the question carefully and look for clues. Watch particularly for adjectives and nouns describing difficult terms or words that you don't recognize. Regardless of if you completely understand a word or not, replacing it with a synonym either provided or one you more familiar with may help you to understand what the questions are asking. Rather than wracking your mind about specific detailed information concerning a difficult term or word, try to use mental substitutes that are easier to understand.

The Trap of Familiarity

Don't just choose a word because you recognize it. On difficult questions, you may not recognize a number of words in the answer choices. The test writers don't put "make-believe" words on the test; so don't think that just because you only recognize all the words in one answer choice means that answer choice must be correct. If you only recognize words in one answer choice, then focus on that one. Is it correct? Try your best to determine if it is correct. If it is, that is great, but if it doesn't, eliminate it. Each word and answer choice you eliminate increases your chances of getting the question correct, even if you then have to guess among the unfamiliar choices.

Eliminate Answers

Eliminate choices as soon as you realize they are wrong. But be careful! Make sure you consider all of the possible answer choices. Just because one appears right, doesn't mean that the next one won't be even better! The test writers will usually put more than one good answer choice for every question, so read all of them. Don't worry if you are stuck between two that seem right. By getting down to just two remaining possible choices, your odds are now 50/50. Rather than wasting too much time, play the odds. You are guessing, but guessing wisely, because you've been able to knock out some of the answer choices that you know are wrong. If you are eliminating choices and realize that the last answer choice you are left with is also obviously wrong, don't panic. Start over and consider each choice again. There may easily be something that you missed the first time and will realize on the second pass.

Tough Questions

If you are stumped on a problem or it appears too hard or too difficult, don't waste time. Move on! Remember though, if you can quickly check for obviously incorrect answer choices, your chances of guessing correctly are greatly improved. Before you completely give up, at least try to knock out a couple of possible answers. Eliminate what you can and then guess at the remaining answer choices before moving on.

Brainstorm

If you get stuck on a difficult question, spend a few seconds quickly brainstorming. Run through the complete list of possible answer choices. Look at each choice and ask yourself, "Could this answer the question satisfactorily?" Go through each answer choice and consider it independently of the other. By systematically going through all possibilities, you may find something that you would otherwise overlook. Remember that when you get stuck, it's important to try to keep moving.

Read Carefully

Understand the problem. Read the question and answer choices carefully. Don't miss the question because you misread the terms. You have plenty of time to read each question thoroughly and make sure you understand what is being asked. Yet a happy medium must be attained, so don't waste too much time. You must read carefully, but efficiently.

Face Value

When in doubt, use common sense. Always accept the situation in the problem at face value. Don't read too much into it. These problems will not require you to make huge leaps of logic. The test writers aren't trying to throw you off with a cheap trick. If you have to go beyond creativity and make a leap of logic in order to have an answer choice answer the question, then you should look at the other answer choices. Don't overcomplicate the problem by creating theoretical relationships or explanations that will warp time or space. These are normal problems rooted in reality. It's just that the applicable relationship or explanation may not be readily apparent and you have to figure things out. Use your common sense to interpret anything that isn't clear.

Prefixes

If you're having trouble with a word in the question or answer choices, try dissecting it. Take advantage of every clue that the word might include. Prefixes and suffixes can be a huge help. Usually they allow you to determine a basic meaning. Pre- means before, post- means after, pro - is positive, de- is negative. From these prefixes and suffixes, you can get an idea of the general meaning of the word and try to put it into context. Beware though of any traps. Just because con is the opposite of pro, doesn't necessarily mean congress is the opposite of progress!

Hedge Phrases

Watch out for critical "hedge" phrases, such as likely, may, can, will often, sometimes, often, almost, mostly, usually, generally, rarely, sometimes. Question writers insert these hedge phrases to cover every possibility. Often an answer choice will be wrong simply because it leaves no room for exception. Avoid answer choices that have definitive words like "exactly," and "always".

Switchback Words

Stay alert for "switchbacks". These are the words and phrases frequently used to alert you to shifts in thought. The most common switchback word is "but". Others include although, however, nevertheless, on the other hand, even though, while, in spite of, despite, regardless of.

New Information

Correct answer choices will rarely have completely new information included. Answer choices typically are straightforward reflections of the material asked about and will directly relate to the question. If a new piece of information is included in an answer choice that doesn't even seem to relate to the topic being asked about, then that answer choice is likely incorrect. All of the information needed to answer the question is usually provided for you, and so you should not have to make guesses that are unsupported or choose answer choices that require unknown information that cannot be reasoned on its own.

Time Management

On technical questions, don't get lost on the technical terms. Don't spend too much time on any one question. If you don't know what a term means, then since you don't have a dictionary, odds are you aren't going to get much further. You should immediately recognize terms as whether or not you know them. If you don't, work with the other clues that you have, the other answer choices and terms provided, but don't waste too much time trying to figure out a difficult term.

Contextual Clues

Look for contextual clues. An answer can be right but not correct. The contextual clues will help you find the answer that is most right and is correct. Understand the context in which a phrase or statement is made. This will help you make important distinctions.

Don't Panic

Panicking will not answer any questions for you. Therefore, it isn't helpful. When you first see the question, if your mind goes blank, take a deep breath. Force yourself to mechanically go through the steps of solving the problem and using the strategies you've learned.

- 155 -

Pace Yourself

Don't get clock fever. It's easy to be overwhelmed when you're looking at a page full of questions, your mind is full of random thoughts and feeling confused, and the clock is ticking down faster than you would like. Calm down and maintain the pace that you have set for yourself. As long as you are on track by monitoring your pace, you are guaranteed to have enough time for yourself. When you get to the last few minutes of the test, it may seem like you won't have enough time left, but if you only have as many questions as you should have left at that point, then you're right on track!

Answer Selection

The best way to pick an answer choice is to eliminate all of those that are wrong, until only one is left and confirm that is the correct answer. Sometimes though, an answer choice may immediately look right. Be careful! Take a second to make sure that the other choices are not equally obvious. Don't make a hasty mistake. There are only two times that you should stop before checking other answers. First is when you are positive that the answer choice you have selected is correct. Second is when time is almost out and you have to make a quick guess!

Check Your Work

Since you will probably not know every term listed and the answer to every question, it is important that you get credit for the ones that you do know. Don't miss any questions through careless mistakes. If at all possible, try to take a second to look back over your answer selection and make sure you've selected the correct answer choice and haven't made a costly careless mistake (such as marking an answer choice that you didn't mean to mark). This quick double check should more than pay for itself in caught mistakes for the time it costs.

Beware of Directly Quoted Answers

Sometimes an answer choice will repeat word for word a portion of the question or reference section. However, beware of such exact duplication – it may be a trap!

More than likely, the correct choice will paraphrase or summarize a point, rather than being exactly the same wording.

Slang

Scientific sounding answers are better than slang ones. An answer choice that begins "To compare the outcomes…" is much more likely to be correct than one that begins "Because some people insisted…"

Extreme Statements

Avoid wild answers that throw out highly controversial ideas that are proclaimed as established fact. An answer choice that states the "process should be used in certain situations, if…" is much more likely to be correct than one that states the "process should be discontinued completely." The first is a calm rational statement and doesn't even make a definitive, uncompromising stance, using a hedge word "if" to provide wiggle room, whereas the second choice is a radical idea and far more extreme.

Answer Choice Families

When you have two or more answer choices that are direct opposites or parallels, one of them is usually the correct answer. For instance, if one answer choice states "x increases" and another answer choice states "x decreases" or "y increases," then those two or three answer choices are very similar in construction and fall into the same family of answer choices. A family of answer choices is when two or three answer choices are very similar in construction, and yet often have a directly opposite meaning. Usually the correct answer choice will be in that family of answer choices. The "odd man out" or answer choice that doesn't seem to fit the parallel construction of the other answer choices is more likely to be incorrect.